A Snapshot of the 1940s

Paul Lyng

Dedication

I decided to write this book the day I received my Benemerenti Papal Award for my work in Booterstown Church. It is in remembrance of the people of Booterstown, the people I grew up with and the characters I met over the years, who were often never remembered for their good deeds and community spirit.

To these folk, and in their memory, I dedicate this award.

BOOTERSTOWN

A Snapshot of the 1940s

Let's go on a journey.

So here we are about to board the steam train at Amiens Street station. Off we go, bound for Booterstown, crossing Butt Bridge. We look down at the river Liffey. We go through Tara Street and Pearse Street stations, then we continue as far as Sydney Parade and on to Merrion Gates. Suddenly, we can see the sea and a lovely view of the hill of Howth as the train steams into Booterstown station.

The year is 1942. As you alight the train, looking out to sea, the tide is out; you can see lots of birds such as geese; ducks and oyster catchers. What's that on the fifth bank, is it a flock of puffins?

Yes, it is.

These birds disappeared around the early 1950s. Why did they go? Will they ever return?

I don't know.

Now we walk across the bridge leaving the station. You might see my dad, especially if its 8:30 a.m. He will be boarding the train with his friends from Booterstown, Roy Mulleady, Paddy Dundon and Patricia Morrison; they all get into the same carriage together; my dad opens his newspaper and reads out for all to hear the breaking news of the day about Curly Wee and Goosey Goose.

As I leave the station on the right side I see the Station Master's house where my good friend Desie Murphy grew up as a young boy, a place where my brother, Paschal and I had great fun with all our friends in Desie's garden, down by the river. We also had fun in the station's bicycle room.

On the left side, look over the wall and you will see the pond. The tide is out, there is a distinctive smell rising from the pond and also from the land-fill at the circus field, now known as Booterstown Park. Looking toward the city you will see Lewis's field, as it was known then.

Booterstown Nature Reserve

Looking further on, there is a white building with a neon sign clock; this is called IMCO, a dry cleaning factory. Looking down over the wall, on the right hand side, about twelve feet below the car park you can see small parcels of land, called plots or allotments, where people grew potatoes and vegetables, during World War 11 – the Emergency – as it was known in Ireland.

At the top of the Station Road there was a confectionary shop, run by my grandfather, Thomas Lyng, in the mid 1880s. Later on it was well-known as Kinch's shop.

In this photograph from right to left is my mother, my father, my aunt Marion, my uncle Edward, my grandmother, my aunt Jane and the man in the doorway is my cousin, Tom Lyng.

We have now arrived at the junction of Booterstown Avenue and the Rock Road; look out for trams coming from left and right. Before we cross the road, let's go forward to the year 1943. Mr. Lewis was a dairy-farmer then in Merrion; he used the field that is now Booterstown Marsh for his cows during the summer months. Later that year, a very wet autumn was followed by a severe winter and water lodged on Lewis's field (now the Marsh) and during the winter it froze.

I saw people ice-skating there; one of them may have been Mr. Maurice Neligan, a young boy, who at that time lived on St. Helen's Road. He told me about his ice-skating episodes on Lewis's field. Later he became one of the first heart-transplant surgeons in Ireland. Sadly,

Maurice died at the time of writing this book; he is very much missed by his wife, Pat and family and his many friends – may he rest in peace.

My friends and I played football here in Lewis's field; we chased the cows to one end of the field and put our coats down as markers for the goal-posts, enjoying some lively games there.

Now, let us return to the Rock Road; looking towards the city, beside the nature reserve sign there was a tram stop; a phone box and a horse trough. On looking the other direction, at Willow Park gates, there was also a tram stop and a horse trough. These horse troughs were placed throughout the city as all deliveries of goods in the city were made by horse-drawn vans. The horses were very, big, working-animals, mostly Clydesdales; they needed to drink quite a lot of water.

Where the bicycle shop is now, there was a butcher's shop run by Mr. Gerard Doyle. Next door to the butcher's was Francis P. McMahon, Chemist and upstairs, Tommy Basquille, the baker of beautiful cakes and brown bread. On the corner was Cassidy's high-class grocer, which has since been demolished.

From left: my father Tom Lyng, my grandmother, my aunt Marion, and my uncle Edward

The Punch Bowl was on the other corner. The corner of this building was No. 1 Booterstown Ave, where my grandfather opened a confectionary shop in the year 1890; this is where my father, my uncle and my aunt were born in 1892, 1893 and 1895 respectively.

My great, great, grandfather is pictured here with my father

My dad told me that when he was about five years of age, he peeped through a curtain into the living room and saw James Connolly standing beside the mantle-piece with a glass in his hand, singing *Annie Laurie*. James was a regular visitor to my grandfather's home, along with other republicans, all relatives of my grandfather.

James Connolly was born in Edinburgh on 5th June, 1868. He spent seven years in the King's

Liverpool Regiment, after which he became a socialist activist. He came to Dublin in 1896, where he founded the Irish Republican Socialist Party.

The names of the founding members of that Party are: James Connolly, Robert Dorman, Tom and Murtagh Lyng, John Moore, Patrick Cushan, Alex Kennedy and Peter Kavanagh.

James Connolly (seated, fourth from left) pictured with local men

This photograph taken in the Phoenix Park shows a group of I.R.S.P. members, which was first published in the Irish Times, on 12th May, 1956
Front row, from left: John Arnall, EW Stewart, Thomas Brady, James Connolly, John J. Lyng, William O'Brien and John Carolan
Back row, from left: W.J. Bradshaw, John Branigan, J. Goff, Mark Deering, Murtagh J. Lyng, Daniel O'Brien, Thomas J. Lyng and James Bishop

My dad also told me another story which occurred on Monday, 1st May, 1916, reported in the *Evening Herald* in the 1960s by Tom Hennigan.

On that Easter Monday, my dad was living in Clanbrassil Street. He was walking along the street with his bicycle. When he finally arrived at St. Stephen's Green it was to hear the staccato rattle of machine guns and shouts of command from the British military. An old woman in a shawl shouted to my dad, to "Come in outa that, ya eejit – d'ya want to get kilt?" That was his introduction to the 1916 Easter Rising. He had no connection with any part of it and he had no idea what was happening.

The woman made him come into her hallway and wait until the military had passed by. After waiting for about one hour, he thanked the old woman and promptly went to stay with his mother in Killiney.

On the Tuesday morning he took the train to Kingstown (now called Dun Laoghaire) to get a newspaper to see if there was any report about the rebellion in the city. A soldier on the train asked him for identification, he showed him his union card which bore his name, Tom Lyng. His first cousin was also Tom Lyng; he was a republican on the wanted list. The soldier thought my dad was the wanted man, so my dad was arrested. He was taken off the train in Dun Laoghaire and marched up Marine Road between two columns of soldiers. The people there, who were very loyalist, shouted obscenities and called him a murderer. He was brought to the police station in Kingstown, where he was interrogated and placed in a cell with some republican prisoners – one of the prisoners was Paddy Moran; my dad struck up a friendship with Paddy.

THE RELUCTANT REBEL

EVENING HERALD SPECIAL

MR. AND MRS. TOM LING

TOM LING, the reluctant rebel of the Easter Rising, looked with pity on the 18-year-old boy seated opposite him on the prison train rumbling its route to Wakefield Jail. The boy stared with vacant eyes. His face was bruised and blackened. A rosary beads hung round his neck. He babbled incoherently. The young soldier had fought in Boland's Mills and now with hundreds of other 1916 men was bound for the English prison.

The plight of the shocked youngster, who died the following night, helped Tom Ling forget for the moment his own desperate situation. For he was one of the innocent caught up in the maelstrom of the Rising—and was to suffer all the rigours of imprisonment and degradation in store for the men who fought in Dublin.

To-day from the eminence of his 74 years, Tom, who lives at 14 Pembroke Cottages, Booterstown, looks back not in anger but in tolerant reminiscence at his exciting but frightening experiences of that fateful time.

It was the Kish lightship's last tour of duty on the Kish Bank which jogged the memory of Tom Ling—for on the Tuesday of Easter Week he found himself crowded into the 'tween decks already cramped with hundreds of prisoners taken in the round-up of suspects. The Kish was pressed into service as a temporary prison while she lay in the harbour at Dun Laoghaire for servicing.

Swept along

The events since Monday were so rapid that Tom wondered if he was not dreaming. Like a drowning man caught in the vortex of a whirlpool he was swept along in the current of the Rising—but it was no nightmare. It was six weeks later when he stepped a free man once more ashore at Dun Laoghaire. His friends or his family never knew where he had been.

Tom was 24 that Easter. An assistant in a pawnbroking shop in Glanbrassil St., his main concern on Easter Tuesday was to get in to work before 8 a.m. Trains were disrupted but he knew little about the events of the previous day in Dublin. He was staying with friends in Killiney and on Easter Monday there were only vague rumours of "trouble" in the city reaching the holidaymakers at the seaside resorts.

When he finally got in to Stephen's Green it was to hear the staccato rattle of machine guns and the shouts of command of British military. An old woman in a shawl shouted to him—to "come in outa that ya cejit —d'ya want to get kilt." That was his introduction to the Easter Rising. About the preparations for it he knew nothing. He had no connection with any of the organisations taking part in it.

Misfortune

Back in Dun Laoghaire on Tuesday he went down to get a newspaper to read about the rebellion. He didn't come back for six weeks. With hundreds of others he was hauled up in the net at Dun Laoghaire barracks, had the misfortune to tell an R.I.C. man that he was a first cousin of Tom Ling, the friend of James Connolly and co-founder of the Socialist Republic party. To the authorities that was enough to "hang" Tom.

That evening he was taken out to the Kish lightship and packed into the 'tween decks. Crammed like sardines in the stench-filled compartments where oil lamps reeked, many of the prisoners were sick. Among them was Tom and a man named Paddy Moran. They were both allowed up on deck. They got violently sick but the following day were attended by a doctor and treated.

Paddy Moran a few years later was to die by execution—after he refused to take his chance to escape from Kilmainham Jail with Simon Donnelly, Ernie O'Malley and Teeling. He felt he owed something to the witnesses who came forward to prove his innocence of the charges against him. His faith in British justice was sadly misplaced.

By Wednesday Tom Ling was in Richmond Barracks where hundreds of the rebels were in captivity. Here there was no mercy for Irishmen. Brutal troops kept the prisoners enclosed for three days before one courageous volunteer named Finn looked unflinchingly into the barrels of two guns in the hands of two soldiers who threatened to shoot him on the spot, and refused to back down until permission to go out had been given.

Guards on the doors shamelessly took money from desperate prisoners seeking food, clothes or trying to send messages to friends and never came back.

Songs

The rebels sang battle songs, their spirits were unquenched but for Tom Ling, who had no such reserves of spirit or strength to fall back on, this was a nightmarish situation. Yet he was able to look impartially on what took place. He recalls the young soldiers rushing to the windows to watch their officers and comrades cross the parade ground to and from the court martials.

Before the executions began Tom and his fellow prisoners were to be herded into the stinking holds of a cattle boat, left in darkness, with hatches battened down and transported to England. It was Friday of Easter Week. The night before Franciscan priests were allowed into the barracks to hear Confessions. For many prisoners it was their last.

On the train to Wakefield Prison Tom tried to help the 18-year-old who over in Boland's Mills. It was no use. The boy was too far gone. The night after they entered the prison he died in the cell next to Tom's. He never found out who he was.

Before his term of trial was over Tom Ling was to know the harsh laws of the English prison system, the hostility of the warders to the Irish cause, the poor food and the bitter humiliation of scrubbing cells and corridors, of being watched day and night, of being caged like an animal.

He will always remember the spirit of the rebels. There was the day when an innocent young English priest at Mass in the prison very seriously lectured them on the necessity for observing His Majesty's Prisons' Regulations —he was greeted with a vociferous rendering of "Hail, Glorious St. Patrick."

The executions were over in Dublin, the city was in ruins and the people dispirited when, after a month in Wakefield, Tom Ling with other prisoners was given his ticket to Holyhead and arrived home again at Dun Laoghaire.

To-day the reluctant rebel is retired from the pawnbroking business and lives happily tending to his duties as parish clerk in Booterstown. He and his wife celebrate their 50th wedding anniversary soon. They have ten children.

Evening Herald report

That evening they were taken to the Kish Lightship, which was used as a temporary prison and packed into the tween decks, crammed like sardines in the stench-filled compartments where oil lamps reeked. My dad and Paddy Moran became violently sick. The next day they were attended by a doctor who gave them a glass of white liquid which tasted horrible, but it was a miraculous cure.

Kish Lightship

By Wednesday of that week they were all interned in Richmond Barracks where hundreds of rebels were in captivity. Here, there was no mercy for Irishmen. Brutal troops kept the prisoners enclosed for three days before one courageous volunteer named Finn looked unflinchingly into the barrels of two guns, in the hands of a British officer, who threatened to shoot him on the spot. He refused to back down, until permission to go out had been given. Guards on the doors, shamelessly, took money from desperate prisoners seeking food, clothes, or trying to send messages to friends and never came back to assist them.

Marine Road, Kingstown – circa 1901

The rebels sang battle songs; their spirits were unquenched. My dad recalled the young soldiers rushing to the windows to watch their officers and comrades cross the parade-ground to and from the Court Martials. Before the executions began, my dad and his fellow prisoners were herded into the stinking, holds of a cattle boat, left in darkness, with hatches battened down and transported to England. It was Friday of Easter week.

The night beforehand, Franciscan priests were allowed into the barracks to hear confessions. For many prisoners it was their last.

On the train to Wakefield prison, my dad tried to help an eighteen year old boy, who had fought in Boland's Mills. He had rosary-beads around his neck. The boy stared with vacant eyes; his face was bruised and blackened; he babbled incoherently, and now with hundreds of other 1916 men, was bound for the English prison. My dad could do nothing for him; the boy was too far gone. The night after they entered the prison, he died in the cell, next to my dad's.

Before his term of trial was over, my dad was to know the harsh laws of the English, prison system, the hostility of the warders to the Irish cause, the poor food, the bitter humiliation of scrubbing cells and corridors, of being watched day and night, of being caged like an animal.

The executions were over in Dublin, the city was in ruins and the people were dispirited. After six weeks in Wakefield, my dad was released. He was given his ticket to Holyhead and arrived home again in Kingstown. It took my dad a long time to get his papers.

A few years later, Paddy Moran died by execution, after he refused to take his chance to escape from Kilmainham Gaol; he felt he owed something to the witnesses who came forward to prove his innocence of the charges against him. His faith in British justice was sadly misplaced. He was later honoured when his name was given to Moran Park in Dun Laoghaire.

On the other side of the Punchbowl, lived Pat and John Flynn, with their wives. Both of these men were collectors and stewards, for many years in our parish church. Next door to them lived the McCarthy family; they had two boys, Justin and James. I think they were twins; they looked like twins, they may have had a sister, I'm not sure, the boys were members of the Legion of Mary. One of the boys, Justin joined the Cistercian Order in Mount Melleray.

On the other side of Grotto Lane, lived Mr. and Mrs. Horan, they had five kerry blue dogs. Mr. Horan used to bring them for walks along the edge of the landfill dump; they were very, vicious dogs but they were great for catching rats.

Mr. Joseph Glennon lived at Glena, in the year 1897 and moved to Booterstown Avenue sometime later. Mr. P.J. Brady lived there until he died in 1943. This man was an Irish Party

MP from 1910 to 1918; he was also a solicitor. He added an oratory to his house and he was given special permission to keep the Blessed Sacrament in a tabernacle in the oratory. The tabernacle is now on one of the side altars in the Church of Our Lady Queen of Peace, Merrion Road. Count John McCormack came to live in Glena in that same year, almost at the end of his singing career. He used to attend the 12 o'clock Mass on Sundays in our parish church, dressed in a black Homburg hat and a Crombie coat with a white silk scarf; he was a very distinguished-looking gentleman. When the choir was singing he also joined in, he died on 16th September, 1945.

This photograph taken at Count John McCormack's funeral outside the Church of the Assumption, Booterstown Ave. shows Mr. Eamon de Valera, Taoiseach in attendance

John McCormack had a grand-daughter, Carol Ann McCormack who is (at the time of writing) a member of the present parish choir, under the baton of Grace Lyons, with Kevin Sheldrick, organist.

Mr. and Mrs. Michael and Jennifer Semple are living in Glena now; Michael is the chairman of the parish finance committee. Next door to Glena is a house called St. Michael's. Living there, at the turn of the century, was a Mr. J.A. Merry. Mr Leo Lynch, a gynaecologist, came to live there with his wife, in the early 1970s. He delivered my second daughter, Martina. Next along this stretch of the Rock Road is No. 130, called Rosevilla, which was owned by a cousin of Mrs. Margaret McGahon, Canon William Field. Leon O'Broin rented this house in 1932, from the Canon. Margaret's aunt went to live there in 1957 and Margaret and her husband, Donal live there now.

Living next door in No. 132 was Mr. and Mrs. Jimmy and Ethel Montgomery and now Mr. and Mrs. James and Ann Montgomery and family: Simon, John, James the lesser, and their daughter, Ruth. It is said that Arthur Griffith used this address as a safe house, during troubled times and other distinguished visitors here were George Orwell and Jack Yeats.

Mr. and Mrs. David Neligan and family lived on St. Helen's Road, as well as Mr. and Mrs. Peter and Greta Clarke and their family, Deirdre, Eimir, Peter, Eoin and Martin. Martin was ordained to the priesthood by Archbishop Dermot Ryan on 20th June, 1980. It was the first ordination in our parish church. At the time of writing this book, Father Martin has been appointed Parish Priest of Donnybrook parish and I wish him well in his new parish. Mr. and Mrs. Herbert Pembrey and family were living here at that time too, they later moved to their newly built house in Glenvar, off Cross Avenue. Mr. Johnny and Mrs. Peggy Claffey and their daughters, Una and Fionnuala were also living here. Next, living here was Mr. and Mrs. Charles Ball and their son. This house and family featured on a programme by Cahal O' Shannon on R.T.E. *Famous Murders*. It was a case of matricide, where a son killed his mother: I won't go into the details.

Mr. E.R. Lee was also living on St. Helen's Road. Next to him were Mr. Nicholas Davin and his family. Then there was Mr. Michael Staines, Mr. C.E. Digges, Peace Commissioner, Mr. and Mrs. Dunne, Dr. T. Hanna, Captain Carew, Mr. and Mrs. Brian O'Brolacháin and family, Cilian, Cormac, Padraig, Manus and Angus. Their son Cormac was ordained a priest in the Spiritan Teaching and Missionary Order (Holy Ghost Fathers), Blackrock College; he is now the President of the college. Also living here were Mr. and Mrs. Sean and Pat Neligan and their family, Margo, Betty and their son, Maurice – as already mentioned – sadly, Maurice died at the time of writing this book.

Mr. Patrick Brett also lived here along with Mr. and Mrs. Davies and their family and Mr. and Mrs. Hally and their sons, Brendan and Desmond; Brendan was ordained a priest in the Spiritan Teaching and Missionary Order, Blackrock College. Living here also were Mr. and Mrs. Cusack and their family, Betty, Patsy, Catherine and Dina.

Mr. and Mrs. Alexander Thompson and their family, daughters, Una and Maureen and son Brendan also lived here. Mr. Stephen and Mrs. Lily Cloonan and their sons, James, Austin and Paddy and daughters, Lily and Beatrice were living here in the 1940s.

In the early forties there were only a few houses in Trimleston. Mr. and Mrs. Beatty and their daughter, Irma, who attended St. Anne's convent school, moved into their new house in Trimleston.

Irma Beatty with her cookery class (front row, second from left)

Canon Flanagan pictured here with Irma Beatty with boys and girls from the parish of the Assumption, Booterstown on her First Holy Communion day.

Mr. and Mrs. David Munro and their large family were also living here, as was Mr. and Mrs. Smyth and their two sons, Brendan and Denis; indeed, they both attended St. Anne's convent school at the same time as me. In 1949, Mrs. Elizabeth Tennent and her daughters, Maureen and Catherine, moved into their new house, in Trimleston. Slowly, but surely, Trimleston, Seafield, Glenomena, Woodbine, and Nutley Lane were built on; but it was into the 1950s before they were complete.

During these war years in the 1940s, there was an invasion of fleas into Ireland; every household had them. Most of the people were not prepared to admit it. I watched, as my mother checked the bed clothes and the mattresses, each morning with a basin of water to drown the fleas that she caught; these fleas were fit for the Olympic Games they could jump 25 feet into the air without a pole for vaulting. As my dad was a pawnbroker and my brother, Tommy was a pawnbroker's apprentice we got it worse than most people, because they took in 1800 articles on a Monday morning, which were mostly clothes, infested with fleas. When my dad and Tommy came home from work, the fleas were hiding in the turn-ups of their trousers; when my mom wasn't looking they sneaked into the beds!

Other problems during the 1940s included an outbreak of scabies – which was not to be mentioned! All families in Dublin had to report in to the Ivy Baths for a sulphur bath and white washing, yes, white washing! So we reported in – that is to say, my dad, my brother, Paschal and I, reported in. We were ushered into a cubicle where there was a bath, filled with brown stuff, which I assume was sulphur; we got into the bath with my dad for about fifteen minutes. Then we stood outside the door of the cubicle, stark naked, my brother and I broke our hearts laughing, but my poor, dad was very embarrassed. A man with a white coat and a bucket-full of white stuff and a brush, painted us all over, really, all over. We then had to get dressed with this white stuff all over us and go home in the tram, smelling like a hospital. The only good thing about this escapade was that none of us got scabies. (The rest of the family went into the Ivy Baths at other times).

Quite a number of households did not attend for treatment, so some of them caught the scabies, (pride must take a fall)! It must be remembered, of course, that at this time, the majority of houses in Ireland had no bathrooms or water inside the house. In our case there was a tap in the yard and an outside toilet. Every Saturday night, the aluminium bath was brought in and filled with hot water – which was a big job in itself – we all had our baths using carbolic soap. When I got into the bath, it was very hot and sometimes, it would burn your bottom, so a bit of a scalding was on the cards. Yes, I did come out of the ark! The other plague of the 1940s was tuberculosis. Whole families were wiped out, before they found a way to deal with the disease, as it was highly contagious. This was a very, sad time for many families in Booterstown and indeed, in the rest of Ireland. The only way to treat it was with antibiotics, putting patients into isolation and ensuring they got plenty of fresh air. Because of this, large, wooden huts were built in places like Crooksling in Brittas, near Blessington, Peamount in Co. Dublin and Newcastle in Co. Wicklow; they were called sanatoriums and after this scheme was introduced, many people survived the illness. At this time they also introduced compulsory screening in the schools; the X-ray van came around to each school and every pupil had to have an X-ray. There was a boy sitting beside me in school, who told me he was coughing up blood and had no intention of going for his X-ray, so I told the nurse in the van about him; I felt like an awful snitch. He was taken away to Peamount; he spent two years there, so I am very glad he survived.

Now let us return to Grotto Lane, as it was then called. You can see the Boys' National

School – the school around the corner – where Bucky Devine was a legendary, schoolmaster; the boys made up a rhyme about him:

Bucky Devine is full of grace
He went to Mass on Sunday
He said his prayers and went to bed
And slaughtered the boys on Monday

Boys' National School, Booterstown
Now the Parish Youth Club

Now I am remembering the people of Grotto Lane: The Corcoran family, the father, Frank was a professional photographer, a real character, well-known as a daily, Mass goer at the 10 o'clock Mass, in our parish church. He told me he was present when Queen Victoria passed by in her carriage in the year 1910.

At that time, there were a number of structures around Dublin and county which were very decorative, using wrought iron and typically English. They were public toilets; there was one of these in Williamstown, so Frank climbed on to the top of this toilet, waving and swinging a Billy can, he lost his balance and fell into it. Thankfully, only his pride was hurt!

Mr. and Mrs. Devitt and their family were well known. Their sons were altar servers. Mr. and Mrs. Finnegan and their family lived here with their son, Cyril; he was an altar server in our parish church and now lives in Chicago, U.S.A; they also had a daughter called Betty. Mr. and Mrs. Walsh and their family, Billy and Olga were also well known in Grotto Lane. Jack Nolan, a World War 1 veteran, repaired boots and shoes, at that time. Jack's relatives, Mr. and Mrs. Johnstone and their family, Reggie, the only son and his two sisters, Olga and Patricia came here to live there, after Jack died.

Reggie, a gentle and very obliging person, was a collector and a steward in our parish church for many years. Mr. and Mrs. Reid and their large family of 12 were living next door to them. I think we must especially remember Johnny Reid, who passed away, at the time of writing this book. We always had great fun with Johnny in the Booterstown Youth Club and at various venues around the city where we took part in Catholic Youth Council activities – performing and competing.

John Sills and his family were also living here; John was a church collector; Mr. and Mrs. Murphy and their family were living here also; the dad and mum and their son, Matt.

My maternal grandparents lived here, my mother, my uncle and my aunts also lived in Grotto Lane until the year 1902. They kept turkeys, geese, hens, goats and a horse. My grandfather owned a feton (a horse drawn carriage); he used it to drive the aristocracy to venues around the city and county. At one time, my grandmother would not allow him to drive anymore; she considered it was too dangerous, especially because he was very fond of a tipple. Really, Albert Einstein was right with his theory that everything is relative to the situation you find yourself in, at any given time, because when they moved to No. 14 Pembroke Cottages, where my five sisters, four brothers and I were born – the house where I still live – they brought everything with them, except the feton and the horse.

At the end of Grotto Lane there was a gate which led into the convent fields; there was a lodge at the gate, where Mr. and Mrs. Morgan and their family lived; their son, Jimmy was an altar server and played for St. Bridget's football team.

St. Bridget's Football Team Sirca 1952

Now, I think I have covered all the people who lived at Grotto Lane. At this time, St. Helen's Road was about ten years built. Trimleston had a few houses built at the Merrion Road side of the parish; Seafield, Woodbine and Nutley Lane were still fields, as was Elm Park Golf Club and where St. Vincent's Hospital now stands; I think in fact, where the hospital is was the 18th green.

Next to the Punch Bowl on Booterstown Avenue, there was an entrance, with a drive into an eighteenth century building; it was the Booterstown Metropolitan Police Station. Serious crime was a major issue in Booterstown at the time; for example, people were riding their bicycles without a lamp, at night. My sister was caught riding her bicycle on Cross Avenue without her lamp and she had to attend court and was fined a half crown – a lot of money in those days. Other serious crime was playing football and cricket on the road. Places like Beech Grove, Pembroke Cottages and McCabe Villas, were hot beds for this sort of crime. The police station closed in 1949, and all moved to Blackrock; it was the end of an era.

The Legion of Mary moved into the police station with the Youth Club from Gardener's Row. In the basement of the police station there was a cell, where offenders could be kept overnight, now, a snooker table was installed for the Youth Club. Bishop Forristal, at that time, a newly ordained priest, was sent as a chaplain to Sion Hill Convent; he was very interested in the youth club and loved to play snooker. He was full of fun; sometimes, when no one was looking he would move the balls on the table, to suit himself and a row would break out, especially, if my brother, Paschal was playing him; Paschal wouldn't forgive him, too easily.

On the right side of the Avenue at No. 3 lived Mr. Leon and Mrs. Cait O'Broin and their family, Eimear, Coilin, Eithne, Noirin and Blanaid. Mr. O'Broin became Secretary of the Department of Posts & Telegraphs.

The famous author of the lives of the United Irishmen, Dr. Richard Madden was living in this house circa 1860; he died in 1886 and was a great friend of Booterstown parish. Living at No. 5, next door, was Mrs. Catherine Powell. In the mid 1930s, living in No. 7 was the owner of these four houses Miss Jessie Leech and in the early 1940s the house was occupied by Mr. and Mrs. Kealy and their sons, John, who became a priest and William and their daughter, Anne; indeed, Anne is still living in the parish. In the early 1930s, Dr. Thomas O'Mahony lived in No. 7 and in the mid 1940s Mr. Pave Brady is recorded as living in No. 9.

Now, let's go to the paper shop run by Frances Timmons and Maggie Kelly. I walked into the shop one day and stood at the counter, the ladies did not come out to serve unless it was absolutely necessary and so this is what I heard: "who's that young fella, Maggie?" "That's young Lyng, Frances." "Oh, which of them is he?" "That's the youngest of them now, she won't be having any more, she's 50 now...." "What do you want?" "I want a chocolate marshmallow." "They are 2d, have you got 2d?" "Yes." "Well, put your 2d on the counter, take your marshmallow and go straight home."

I went over to the box with the marshmallows and there was a very big cat lying on top of the marshmallows with his paws tucked in – I had a big cat myself so I wasn't afraid of him – so I put my hand underneath the cat and fished out my marshmallow, I dusted off the cats hairs and scoffed up the marshmallow – two minutes of absolute pleasure!

The next shop was a fish monger, Billy Pim and his wife. This was a very important shop, at that time, because Fridays were called fast days; it was forbidden to eat meat, so Billy was there to keep us on the straight and narrow, as it was a mortal sin to eat meat on a Friday. The fast day wasn't fast enough! A lot of people waited until after midnight to have a big fry up.

Right next door was the Post Office. When you went in there it was like stepping into a Charles Dickens' novel. Miss Annie Casey and her sister – two lovely old-world ladies ran the Post Office, as well as a high-class confectionary shop which was quite expensive at the time.

One day while I was in the shop, a lad I knew came in; he picked out a small box of chocolates and told me it was for his girlfriend's birthday. "How much are these, Miss Casey?" he asked. "That box is 2s-11d, that is two shillings and eleven pennies," he gave her back the chocolates and said, "Give me ten Gold Flake."

William and Margaret Dowse lived at Chestnut Lodge and Mr. and Mrs. John McKenna were living in Pembroke House with their family; John was a member of the local police force.

The shop called Clarke's Newsagent was next. Mr. Joseph Clarke was a lovely old-world gentleman, he was also a tobacconist; I can see him now smoking his pipe. "A penny worth of mixed sweets, Mr. Clarke?" "Here's two, son mix them yourself."

Principal Post Office Charges

IRISH FREE STATE.

LETTERS.
Not exceeding 3 oz............ 2d.
For every additional oz....... ½d.
Limit : 24 x 12 inches
Registration Fee .... 3d.

BOOK PACKETS.
And other packets of printed matter, 1 oz. or under .... ½d.
1 oz. to 2 oz. .... 1d.
Every additional 2 oz. up to 2 lb. .... ½d.
Limit. 24 x 12 x 12 inches.

NEWSPAPERS. Per copy
6 oz. .... 1d.
For every additional 6 ozs. ½d.
Wrappers Stamped 1d. per pkt. 22 .... 2/-

POST CARDS.
Postage .... 1d.
Stamped Cards, single stout, per pkt. of 7 .... 8½d.
Thin, per pkt. of 11 ...... 1/-

LETTER CARDS.
Stamped, per pkt. of 10 ... 2/-

PARCEL RATES.
Not exceeding 2 lb. .... 6d.
  ,,   ,, 5 ,, ... 9d.
  ,,   ,, 8 ,, ... 1/-
  ,,   ,, 11 ,, ... 1/3
Limit : 11 lbs.; Limit : Length, 3 ft. 6 in.; length and girth, 6 ft.   Receipt (free) insures £2.
Parcels must not be posted in a Letter Box.

POSTAL ORDERS.
Amount of Order. Poundage.
6d. to 2s. 6d. .... 1d.
3s. to 15s. .... 1½d.
16s. to 21s. .... 2d.

INLAND MONEY ORDERS.
Not exceeding £3 .... 4d.
  ,,   ,, £10 .... 6d.
  ,,   ,, £20 .... 8d.
  ,,   ,, £30 .... 10d.
  ,,   ,, £40 .... 1/-

INLAND TELEGRAPH MONEY ORDERS
Poundage at the same rate as for ordinary Inland Money Orders plus supplementary fee of 2d. and cost of official Telegram of advice.

TELEGRAMS.
12 words, 1/6, and every additional word, 1d. Names and addresses of sender and receiver are charged. Free delivery within 1 mile of terminal office.

NIGHT TELEGRAPH LETTERS.
36 words or less, 1/6, and a 1d. for every 3 words beyond 36.

EXPRESS LETTERS.
For local service the charge is 6d. per mile or part of a mile. A reply is charged for at the same rates, except it be taken to an address on the messenger's homeward route or within half a mile of his office, in which case only half the mileage is charged.

RAILWAY LETTERS.
Letters up to 3 oz. are received at any Railway Booking Office or Express Delivery Office, to be called for at Station nearest Address, or posted in nearest Post Office for delivery by Postman. Rates: 2d. stamp and pay 4d. at Booking Office, or if handed in at Express Delivery Office an additional fee of 6d. per mile for despatch to Railway Station.

FOREIGN AND COLONIAL.

LETTERS.
To British Possessions generally. Egypt, the United States of America, British Postal Agencies in Morocco, 2d. for first oz., and 1½d. for each additional oz.
To all other places, 3d. for the first oz., and 1½d. for each additional oz.

NEWSPAPERS.
Per 2 oz. .... ½d.

PRINTED PAPERS, COMMERCIAL PAPERS AND SAMPLES.
Per 2 oz. .... ½d.
Minimum for Commercial Papers .... 3d.
And for Samples .... 1d.

MONEY ORDERS.
British Dominions and certain Foreign Countries, 6d. for every £1 up to £3, and 3d. additional for every £1 over £3

We will now crossover to the other side of Booterstown Avenue to the corner of Cassidy's Grocery Store.

Standing there you might see Pat Hickey from Beech Grove; he always wore a peak cap, smoked a pipe and had one hand behind his back. He used to come every day; it looked like he was part of the corner and you would certainly miss him if he wasn't there. He was one of the special characters of that time.

Mrs. Ellen Doyle lived in No. 2. Mr. and Mrs. Cole and their two daughters lived in No. 4.

Mr. Cole was a chemist; they called their house Journey's End. Next door, at No. 4a, the O'Brien family lived, remembering Violet, Eileen, Dorothy, Cora and her brother, Mick, who was an altar server in our parish church. Miss E. Kirby lived at No. 8; she played the organ in our parish church, for many years. Mr. Sidney Herbert is recorded as having lived in No. 6 in 1901. Mrs. Reilly lived at No. 10 with her daughter, Jenny, who was also the church organist for many years; she was a bit briary, because we, as altar servers were often sent up to the gallery, to pump the air into the organ, by means of a wooden bar, which operated a bellows, if we were slacking on the job in hand, she would bang the side of the organ and shout, "More air, wake up." She would report us to Tom Maguire and say, "Don't send that boy up to pump the organ anymore, he is far too lazy."

Next door were Mr. and Mrs. Grace and their family who lived at No. 16. Their son, Seamus was a teacher in Blackrock College and was president of the Legion of Mary there. The Toft family also lived on this part of the Avenue. My eldest brother, Tommy was a great friend of the Tofts, Willie, John and Tony. Willie joined the Royal Navy and became a Chief Petty Officer. Later on the other two boys also joined up. John was aboard a submarine, called the H.M.S. Salmon, when she was struck by a German torpedo, all on board were lost.

Tony was serving onboard H.M.S. Courageous, an aircraft carrier, when she was struck by a German torpedo, a lot of sailors, including Tony, lost their lives. That week it was all over the newspapers about the two Dublin men, on the Courageous; one was saved but Tony Toft was lost.

Tony Toft

My brother Tommy and some of his friends went to see the surviving man, who lived in Donnybrook. He told them that Tony was below the decks where the torpedo struck; there were no survivors from below decks.

This man said he was saved by a relative of the Royal Family who was an officer on board the Courageous at that time. Willie Toft survived the war and later on went to live in New Zealand.

Next were the Behan family, Tommy and Hannah. Tommy was a member of the famous Behan family who were well known painters in Dublin city. Tommy had a funny nickname –Chickalawinka – don't ask why. The family brought two relatives from Cork to stay with them called Terry and Cecil. Further up, on that side of the road, was the Walsh family. Their son, Tommy was well known to all his peers. Mrs. Muldoon, who was a dressmaker, was in the next house and Mr. Norris, Commanding Officer of the Local Services Forces (L. S. F.), lived right next door to Garvey's Hardware Store, which displayed its goods outside the shop – crockery, buckets, basins,   shovels, spades, cutlery, wooden spoons, etc.

Garvey's Hardware Store

Ernest Ford, the barber was next on the row. His daughter, Madge also became a hairdresser.

Next door to them lived Mr. McCormac; he was a Police Inspector and was well liked by the people of Booterstown, at that time.

In the house just before the wall of Willow Park School lived Gin Dunphy, a sister of Min, Liz and brother, Paddy, who lived in Pembroke Cottages.

A little bit down from here you get a panoramic view of Beech Grove. Midway you can see a large water tank, almost touching the walls on both sides of the road. This tank was built during World War 11 as an emergency water supply.

On hot July days you might have seen some of us swimming in the tank. Happily, the water wasn't for drinking; it was in case of a fire.

Looking further on again, you can see a garden, at what is now the entrance to Castle Court; one section of this garden was managed by Mr. T. Colgan, the great, grand-father of Thomas Colgan, the Assistant Sacristan in our parish church. Every year in the autumn, his chrysanthemums were magnificent.

On the corner of Beech Grove lived Peader Brady and his wife, Maisie with their family Marie and Laura. Beside them lived the Griffin family. Jimmy Griffin was head altar boy during the early 1940s. Later he became Assistant Sacristan. He was also a founder member of the Legion of Mary, who were involved in the setting up of the first boys' and girls' club in the year 1948. Jimmy fell in love with Bridie Byrne; they got married in October 1959 and moved to Newtown Park. They celebrated their Golden Jubilee last year in our parish church – Congratulations Jimmy and Bridie!

Jimmy Griffin and Joe Dalton

The other people living in Beech Grove were as follows: The Coffey family, whose son, John was a powerful swimmer. During those days, a lot of people were drowned in a place called the Cockle Lake, which was out beside the shipping channel. People from the inner city and other visitors would often swim there when the tide was out; they didn't know the danger. The channel was very deep; it was just like stepping off the edge of a cliff. John was often called on to recover the dead bodies; he is now living in Dun Laoghaire and is a very valuable voluntary worker in Dun Laoghaire church. Mr. and Mrs. Mooney and their family lived next door to the Coffey family with their daughter, Geraldine and her brother Morgan, who was a member of our first parish folk group.

The Hennessey family were next; the uncle, Joe was a World War 1 veteran. At this time, he was a night watchman, employed by the council. When they were resurfacing the roads, he had a lovely cosy hut with a brazier, style fire of coke; it glowed in the dark – a very, hot, frosty fire. My companions and I would often go and sit with him and listen to his stories. One story he told us was about milk you could get in a tin, at the time; it was called Kerry milk. It was very thick and creamy; he told us the rats loved it, so to stop the rats getting at his milk he punched a hole in the top of the tin one night. As he was watching, he said, he saw a rat walking across the shelf he put his tail into the hole in the tin and sucked his tail – a very clever rat!

On another occasion, Joe told us how a rat stole his eggs: One night, as he was on watch, a rat went across his shelf and took an egg from the box and then he rolled over onto his back, with the egg on his tummy. Another rat came along and grabbed his tail in his mouth and dragged him away with the egg, enough said!

Joe's nephew, Bill joined the Royal Navy and survived World War 11. The Hennesseys also sold coal, by the stone, in Beech Grove; Paddy Hennessey was the last of the Hennesseys to live in Beech Grove.

Mr. and Mrs. Chuck Kelly and their family were next. Chuck was a leader of the Blackrock Brass and Reed Band, when he died he had the biggest funeral we ever saw in Booterstown parish. There were at least 2,000 people present, the band assembled and led the way. Chuck was carried all way to the church, as was the custom. There were a lot of thirsty people at that funeral and Ned and Sarah Murphy did a great bit of trading that night in their pub; the overflow went down to the Punch Bowl and a great night was had by all. Mr. and Mrs. Corrigan and their sons Billy and Dinny lived in Beech grove at that time. Dinny got married to Teresa and they are still living there, very happily with their family.

Mr. and Mrs. Timmons and family were also living here. Their son, Ned married May Doran from Booterstown Avenue and raised a large family. We also remember Sarah Colgan and her sister, Nell and the Collins family and their son, Jimmy (The Bomber) as well as Thomas Kelly and his wife. Bill Colgan was another old friend who lived here also.

Mr. and Mrs. Grimes were next on the road. Their son, Noel is still living there now with his wife, Laura and their family. Indeed, Mrs. Grimes was a good friend of my mother and ironically, they both died on the same day. Their two coffins were together overnight in our parish church.

Mr. and Mrs. Giles with their family were living in the next house. Their son, Jimmy was a very good footballer as well as an altar server in our parish church. Mr. and Mrs. Peter King and their family were also living here. Peter (Peony) was a war veteran; he told us there was a bullet lodged under his heart. He was wounded in battle and they could not remove it because it was too close to his heart, so he had to live with it all his long life. Mr. and Mrs. Edward (Ned) and Mary (Millie) Printer and family, John, Margaret and Patrick also lived here at the time. Ned Printer was a hackney-man; he had a most, beautiful, Austin12, vintage, hackney, brass headlamps running boards and coach paint. He kept it in immaculate condition. Ned was also an all year around swimmer and a very popular man around our parish. I already mentioned Pat Hickey who also lived there with his family. Then there was Mr. and Mrs. O'Brien and their son, Arthur. We also remember the Keogh family. Last but not least, we remember Thomas Colgan Senior, an altar server for many years and his sister, Kathleen. Tom fell in love with Sheila White from Blackrock; they got married in 1948 and had two children, Valerie and Thomas. Tom was a church collector for over forty years; he also looked after the church grounds for many years with lots of help from his son, Thomas. Tom was a real gentleman and had a great sense of humour, he was very kind and most obliging. He loved to sing old cowboy songs, *Old Faithful* and *Ghost Riders in the Sky*. Sadly, he died at the age of 63 and is missed very much by his family, Sheila, Valerie and Thomas and the rest of us.

Tom's sister, Kathleen worked in Doyle's Butcher Shop on the Rock Road, she got married to Noel Breen and they had two children, Liam and Anthony. They were Kathleen's pride and joy; sadly, she contracted MS, a slow debilitating disease. She bore her cross cheerfully and with great dignity to the end. She was a very saintly person, a real lady.

Now we move out to the house on the corner of Beech Grove. Sean McGarry lived here; he was in Lincoln Jail with Eamon de Valera. They used to serve Mass each morning in the prison chapel. They stole the key to the prison and with candle wax, they got from the chapel sacristy, they made an impression of the key. They gave the wax impression to

Sean's wife, who was able to get a key made. It took a few attempts, she put the key into a baked cake and eventually, the two men escaped. Sadly, they were divided during the civil war.

Back row: Sacristan, Tom Maguire and Assistant Sacristan, Dan Maher
From left: Jim Stone (Later, Parish Priest of Ringsend) Tom Colgan, Patsy
Flanagan, Brendan Timbs and Tommy Corcoran.
(circa 1930 – Blackrock Rail Station)

Next door, Mr. and Mrs. Bourke and their family, Jack, Denis, Morris and Jim who were all altar servers, lived. Morris joined the Royal Navy fleet air arm and became a Radio Officer. Next were Mr. and Mrs. Cuddy and then Mr. and Mrs. Leach who lived with their son, Peter and their daughter. Peter worked in England and was injured in an accident with machinery when he was only 17 years old; he was brought home in an air ambulance. Some time later he was brought to Lourdes, after some years, he recovered to live a fairly, normal life. He became a real character around the town. He had a great interest in marching bands' music, especially, John Philip Souza – an interest I shared with him. Peter moved to Monkstown, and later wound up in a wheel chair before he died there, may he rest in peace.

Next to them lived Mr. and Mrs. Maguire and their family, Kevin and Dermot. Both of the boys were altar servers and like many others before them, they joined the British Armed Forces, the fleet air arm. Along this part of the Avenue lived Gerry McDermot with his family and Mr. and Mrs. Curry with their daughter, Kathleen, who became a marvellous voluntary worker in our parish. At that time, Merrion Road was part of our parish. There was a chapel of ease on Merrion Road, often referred to as the tin church. Kathleen worked tirelessly to collect funds for the building of a new church on Merrion Road. She was involved in non-stop draws, raffles, door-to-door collections and later on, bingo in the hall at St. Vincent's Hospital.

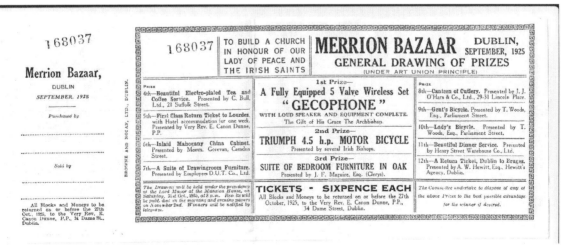

A typical raffle ticket to raise funds for Merrion Church
(this raffle took place in September 1925)

Kathleen was also one of the last surviving members of the Children of Mary at that time. She was also a founder member of the Martha Society of Church Cleaners. Willie Divine came along on his bicycle and swept Kathleen off her feet; they were married in 1943 and had three children, William, Mary and Sylvia.

Willie was a member of the Legion of Mary at that time; he was also a church collector for many years. The next house was occupied by the Stone family. Mr. and Mrs. Stone's sons, Jimmy and Joe were ordained to the priesthood, in the year 1947; their son, John became an architect. They also had a daughter, May who is still living in the family home. Indeed, May is a member of the St. Joseph's Young Priests' Society. I had the privilege of serving Joe's first Mass in our parish church.

Next on the Avenue, lived Mrs. McCormac, known locally as the cat woman. She worked in the cats and dogs home and always had a cigarette in her mouth. It wouldn't be unusual to see her calling to neighbouring houses with a cage to collect unwanted cats or dogs. She was tragically, killed crossing the main road, at the bus stop, on the Rock Road. Her house was full of cats, about thirty in all. The people from the cats and dogs home had an awful job collecting the cats, as some of them had become very wild.

In the next house was Mr. and Mrs. Harlowe, with their sons, Jim, Gerald and David and their daughter, Ann. Mr. Harlowe contracted tuberculosis, so rather than send him to a sanatorium, Mrs. Harlowe got a hut built at the bottom of the garden and Mr. Harlowe moved into the hut with all his own clothing, plates, cutlery, cups, glasses – everything! No direct contact could be made with him. Mrs. Harlowe had a young family; she was a very brave woman to take on this task, she looked after them all very well. In spite of all her good work, the poor man did not survive; no other members of the family got the disease. Jim and Gerald were altar servers. Jim also joined the fleet air arm as a Radio Officer. He is now a collector at the nine o'clock Mass every Sunday.

Next door were Mr. and Mrs. Woods, an English couple, they ran a general store on a small scale.

Mr. Woods had a nick name (Rubber Neck) because he had a long neck, which he could swivel more than most people. He was a very witty man and the owner of a parrot, which escaped once. Mr. Woods put a notice in his shop window which read,

Parrot missing:
Last seen on the telegraph wire
Reciting:
'Buy your goods at Woods'

Another notice he put in his shop window was a sketch of a footballer with a broken leg, which was to the rear. The good leg was at the front, the caption read,

Please help St. Mary's football club
Put your best foot forward

During the war, when people were in the shop looking for goods which were unavailable, Mrs. Woods was known to say, with a very pronounced English accent.

'No cigs, no chocks, no butter, no tea.
You can't have your bun and eat it.'

Mr. Michael O'Callaghan lived next door to the English couple. Then there was Mrs. Catherine Moore and beside Mrs. Moore lived Mr. Thomas Owens. Next to that, is the house with the eagles, called Ashfield House, where Mr. Christopher Glennon lived; his house keeper was Bella Feeney, a very good neighbour and friend around this parish. When my brother, Tommy was getting married in the year 1947, Bella brought Ita, Tommy's fiancée, and Tommy into the rear garden to pick flowers for their wedding in St. Michael's Church, Dun Laoghaire, with of course, Mr. Glennon's approval. Next were Mr. and Mrs. Murphy and their sons, Gerard and James who were both altar servers and their daughter, Mary.

Back Row: Tom Maguire, Michael Byrne, Bob Reynolds
Front Row: Gerard Murphy and James Murphy

The father, Batt was Mr. de Valera's body guard while he was Taoiseach, he would have been known as a 'Broy Harrier' – a term used to describe bodyguards under the leadership of Colonel Broy who was the Commissioner of Police. His daughter, Mary is still living there with her husband Aidan Moriarty. Miss Madge O'Brien lived next door to the Murphy's at that time. Mr Thomas Murphy also lived in one of these houses at that time. Later on, for a time, Rose Kearney lived in one of these houses. Rose was a cleaner in our parish church for some years. The Mercy nuns took her under their wing; they brought her to their nursing home in Rathdrum, Co. Wicklow and looked after her until she died.

Mr. Gilligan, who ran a much needed taxi service also lived here. Then there was the O'Connor family who lived in the next house on the Avenue; Mr. O'Connor was an Inspector on the trams. Right next door were Mr. and Mrs. Lynch and their family, Michael, Charlie, Pat, Frances, Noel, Tommy, Joe, Sean, Tony and last, but not least, Angela, the only girl. These people were our friends as we were growing up, especially, Noel, Joe, Tony and Sean; their father was a Police Inspector – very handy, if we were in any trouble with Sergeant McManus, which wasn't very hard in those days; there's not enough pages in the whole of Dublin to tell all the fun we had together; but just to mention a few of our escapades, one time, Tony, my brother, Paschal and I rode our bicycles along the sea-wall from Booterstown to Blackrock – this is the stuff nightmares are made of; I don't know how we survived and I wouldn't advise anybody to try this stunt; it is very dangerous.

One day, Tony, my brother, Paschal and I were at the sea, the tide was out and we were driving a golf ball, with a number 3 wood driver, when a man came over to us and said, "Lads you're holding the golf club with the wrong grip." He gave us a golf lesson: stance, feet, eye on the ball, swing and grip. He had his own golf bag full of clubs, he was practising too. When he was finished and gone, we said, "Who does he think he is, telling us what to do?" A couple of days later, Tony came running up to our house with the morning paper to show us a photograph of the man who had given us the golf lesson. It was none other than Harry Bradshaw; he had just won the Irish Open – what a nice man he was, to bother with us!

Tony's brother, Michael was killed in the boxing ring in a tragic accident; a jab to the chest stopped his heart and they couldn't revive him; sadly, he died.

Everyone of this family was bristling with brains. In the early 1940s Charlie made a wind-charger to generate electricity; it was also driven by a small, Ford, petrol, engine just in case there was no wind to drive the turbine. This was the first wind-charger in the whole of Europe, at least, that's what I thought and I am sticking to it. At Christmas in 1947, Joe wired up Bob Reynolds' horse and cart wheels, cart shafts and horse; he used a 6-volt car-battery to supply the power, it was a sight to behold. He dressed up in a Santa Claus uniform (he also had the school bell). It was snowing at the time, which made the occasion much more magical. He proceeded to the Convent of Mercy orphanage, ringing his bell, with presents for all the children – a very happy Christmas, for all concerned, including the nuns and all the rest of us.

In subsequent years, Michael Shelly from McCabe's Villas did Santa. Joe did the wiring. I must say, Michael was a very good Santa Claus. After delivering the goods, Michael was seen standing on a box in Murphy's pub, singing a song called, *Hey Joe*. Joe lynch was very pleased with the gesture.

Joe's brother, Pat was a brilliant footballer. He played for Merrion Rangers, who went on to become Shamrock Rovers. Charlie met Moira who was living in Bray at that time, they fell in love and got married and they had six children, Peter, Paula, Patrick, Mark, Clare and Andréa. My own two daughters, Michelle and Martina, became friends with this new Lynch family – a never ending story.

Moira played a very important part in World War 11; she was a member of the Royal Air Force and she was posted to Bletchley Park, where they decoded the various messages that were coming in from the German Command Head Quarters, this played a big part in bringing the war to an end. I could go on and on but I think I will leave it there for now.

Next door is the Convent of Mercy school where my mother brought me at the tender age of six years old. Sr. Madeline welcomed us in. She put her two hands on my face and said, "Oh! I thought he had a beard, he's so old starting school." My mother said, "You won't have to teach him anything, he knows everything, if you want to know anything, ask him."

Here I would like to say a few words about Religious Orders Nuns, Brothers and Priests; all

I can hear lately, is condemnation and never a good report. I have been taught by the Mercy nuns, the Christian Brothers and priests in the College of Industrial Relations at Sandford Road in Ranelagh and by lay people. I have been living close to the church, the convent, St. Helen's Christian Brothers' Novitiate and Blackrock College and mingled with priests, brothers and nuns all my life, I have never experienced, or heard from my friends of any improper conduct from any of these people.

Mrs. Moira Lynch

The Lynch Family

The Sisters of Mercy came to Booterstown in 1838. Shortly after they arrived, in the early 1840s, there was an outbreak of cholera, which left many children without parents, an orphanage and a school was established by the sisters to care for around seventy children. This orphanage was attached to the convent and also doubled as a National School to all the other children in the area. In the year 1872, the State asked the Sisters of Mercy to take on the running of an orphanage to look after children from over-crowded tenements in the inner city of Dublin, so they built St. Anne's school and orphanage; it is now the parish centre. I wonder what would have become of these children without the intervention of the sisters who made a home for them. I would just like to point out that ninety per cent of clergy and people in religious life are very good Christians and a relatively small percentage have let the rest down very badly.

Here, I would like to say to the unfortunate people who were abused, my hope is that God will console you, lift up your hearts, increase your faith and heal the terrible hurt that was inflicted on you. Before St. Paul was converted, he persecuted Christians; he presided over the martyrdom of St. Stephen. The Lord picked this ruthless, terrorist to spread the Gospel – and what a job he did. The following is an excerpt from an Advent reading from Isaiah 29:17-24

> *"That day the eyes of the blind will see, the lowly will rejoice in the Lord even more and the poorest exult in the holy one of Israel, for tyrants shall be no more, and scoffers vanish, and all will be destroyed who are disposed to do evil, those who gossip to incriminate others, those who try at the gate to trip the arbitrator and get the upright persons case dismissed, for groundless reasons."*

– As relevant today as it was all those years ago.

There is a common denominator between the bishops, the priests, the religious and the abused: –fear of the consequences – the abused people were terrified of what might happen to them if they spoke up, fearing no one would believe them and the bishops, priests and religious were terrified that the reputation of the Catholic Church would be damaged. There isn't a business or a bank or a large developer, a politician, a priest, a bishop, a cardinal, or a pope, a broadcaster, anybody in the legal profession, the media, or anybody else in this whole world that hasn't made a mistake or sinned, Jesus said, love one another as I love you, this is the simple message and we should all try to achieve this.

My sister, Dympna was born mentally and physically handicapped in the year 1929. My father and mother already had five other children so it was going to be difficult now, with a disabled child but they coped very well. Four years later they had twins, a boy and a girl; still they carried on coping; a couple of more years later, they had another baby boy – ah, here! Well, now it was really getting difficult, especially since Dympna disappeared almost every day and the neighbours had to organise search parties to look for her. She had also started to experiment on my brother, Paschal. She used to prop him up in a chair, lather his face with my dad's shaving brush and start to shave his face with my dad's cut-throat razor. She cut his face very badly, but he survived OK. On another occasion, she shoved Paschal under the bed with a sweeping brush; she also used to throw cutlery, delph, ornaments and anything she could pick up, over the garden wall.

Then I arrived; it was the last straw! One day after I was born, Dympna went missing for much longer than usual. At 9.00 p.m. when the nuns were going to bed, she was found, fast asleep in the Reverend Mother's bed. Another day, she escaped once again. This time she got into the parish priest's house. She went up a few steps of his stairs and waited. When the Parish Priest, Canon Flanagan was passing by, she jumped on to his back, he almost died of a heart attack, but he survived. Canon Flanagan called to see my mom and dad; he explained to them that after another couple of years it would be impossible to look after Dympna and she would be too old to be accepted into any institution. They had a very difficult decision to make, but in the end it had to be done. Dympna was taken to St. Vincent's on the Navan Road; it was a very sad time for my mom and dad. It may have been better to have let Dympna go when she was three years old. It would have been easier for all concerned. It took Dympna two years to settle in. St. Vincent's was owned and run by the French Sisters of Charity; they were the nuns with the white bonnets, now called the Daughters of Charity.

I was only a baby when my sister left home, so I didn't know her. My father and mother brought my sister, Dorothy and my brothers, Hilary and Paschal and I to see her, I was just four years old. I wasn't prepared for what I was about to see. There were approximately, three hundred, handicapped children, of all ages in a great hall. What I saw was absolute bedlam, the noise was frightening. My sister Dympna was brought in by Sr. Paul. Dympna was all excited to see mom and dad, but she had no time for us. I was so frightened, I can't remember much more.

One of the Sisters from St. Vincent's on the Navan Road, with some poor boys from the inner city.

As the years went by I looked back on this visit and one thing stood out, the love the handicapped people received and it was obvious that they were happy to be there. The Daughters of Charity are of great service to the people of Ireland; they now have at least five places in Dublin and two in Limerick. When they built St. Joseph's in Clonsilla, my sister was sent there with other special ladies from her unit. Again, it took Dympna a while to adjust; it was more difficult for my mom and dad and the rest of us to get to Clonsilla but as always Dympna's welfare was very important to us. The loving care Dympna received from the sisters and the lay staff especially, Bride McMahon was second to none. Dympna was with the Daughters of Charity for sixty-six years of her life; because it was difficult for us to get there, we were allowed to visit at anytime. We went there on different days and times and we always found everything spotlessly clean; it was obvious the loving care that was given. This is a never ending story, special ladies from all over Ireland, at this time, are receiving special loving care from this organisation: God bless them all.

Paul and his sister Dympna

One day when I was six years old, one of my friends asked me would I like to see his brother. I said, "Yes" He brought me into his house while his mum and dad were out. He brought me up a stairs, to a room which he called the gallery. In this room there was a bed in the corner. Sitting on the bed was a little boy, he was a bit older than me; he had white hair and was slightly blue in colour. He was scared of me, at first, but after a while he warmed to me; we shook hands and then my friend told me we had to go, I said, "Goodbye" He waved at me and smiled, I never saw him again. I know he died when he was about 10 years old. His parents were protecting him as he was very fragile; they were afraid he would get hurt both physically and psychologically, so they kept him out of the cruel world, because they loved him so much, I will never forget him.

We should now cross the road opposite Woods' Shop to Willow Park Lodge, where Mr. and Mrs. Nolan lived with their daughter, Cathleen. At that time there was a gate at the lodge where the locals could take a short-cut through Willow Park to Williamstown. When St.

Andrew's College arrived there was a wall built across where the gates were, to stop the two schools from clashing – nothing lasts. Mrs. Sophia Bewley was living in Willow Lodge in1901. Mrs. Roche lives there now. Living in the next house, at that time, was Miss Margaret Lee. Mr. William Overend was living in Park House in 1901 and the Farrell family were living in Park House in the 1940s.

Murphy's public house was next. Ned and Sarah Murphy ran this pub which was, and still is a landmark on Booterstown Avenue. At that time it was a very old-style, country pub. Through the main door, off the Avenue (the only door), there was a partition on each side leading to a counter where they sold groceries such as tea, butter, sugar, bread, sweets and paraffin oil. Yes! They did! Remember there were lots of oil lamps then, as electric power was still only arriving in Booterstown. On the left side of the partition there was a door into the bar, much the way it is today; on the right, there was a door into a snug which was mainly for women, who at that time, would not be seen in the bar. It is said that at the time, it was two pennies for a gallon of porter. I have very fond memories of going into Sarah's for a penny worth of honey bee or a sailor's chew.

Hilary and Paul Lyng to the left of the photograph with Ned and Sarah Murphy's,
now Gleeson's pub to the right-hand side of Booterstown Avenue in 1948

In the year 1954 Mr. and Mrs. Frank and Norah Gleeson purchased the pub from Sarah Murphy, and turned it into one of the best landmark pubs in Dublin. Over fifty years building it up as a well-known and well-run establishment, Frank and Norah have now retired having handed the pub into the capable hands of their daughter, Mary and their two sons, John and Kieran – every good wish to them all.

In beside the pub was Willow Place; the Brown family, the Rath family, the Wall family and the Billington family all lived here. I particularly remember the Billington's son, Anthony. Opposite Willow Place is the parish church; the parishioners of this parish have been walking in through the same entrance now, for three hundred and twenty four years, since 1686, when the first chapel was built on this site. It was demolished in 1811 to make way for the building of the present church.

ST. MARY'S CHURCH, BOOTERSTOWN—Exterior

Very, Rev. James, Canon Breen, 1933.
He was Parish Priest in Booterstown from 1927 to 1939.
(Note the gas lamp outside).

The following special appeal was made by Canon Breen to raise funds, for the construction of a new church on Merrion Road.

An Appeal

THE GROWTH OF GREATER DUBLIN

The gradual growth of Dublin outside the City Boundaries, towards Blackrock, creates the need of another Church for our Parishioners who reside at the extremities of the present Parish of Booterstown, in the direction of the City.

The generous gift of a site comprising over an acre of land in a prominent position on the North side of the Main Road, near Merrion Gates, was gratefully accepted, and plans for a new Church have already been drawn up and approved.

The main building, comprising Nave, Chancel, two Transepts, and a tall graceful spire, will, when erected, present a beautiful and stately appearance; but to bring this desirable event to its full consumation a considerable sum of money will be needed. It is estimated that the complete structure will cost approximately £40,000, towards which just over £7,000 has been subscribed.

A Building Fund has been opened, and further subscriptions will be very gratefully received by the Very Rev. Canon Breen. Persons who desire to bequeath donations for this good work should do so in the name of the Canon, or the Parish Priest of St. Mary's, Booterstown, for the time being, and such gifts will be very greatly appreciated.

Living in the parochial house from 1939 to 1956 was Rev, Paddy, Canon Flanagan p.p. Next door to the church in Number 71, were Mr. and Mrs. Christopher and Elizabeth Blake and their family, Maura, Gerty, Lily and Anna, who is still living there. Mr. Blake was a member of the Police Force. Mrs. Blake was a great accordion player; we loved to listen to the music and laughter of people, as they danced half-sets and old-time waltzes; theirs was a great house for social evenings.

Early in the 1940s Miss J. Knight lived in No. 73. When she passed away, Mr. and Mrs. Nathanial Long lived there with their family, Delores, Eamon, Malcolm, Pauline, Thomas, Margaret and Carmel. Eamon was an altar server in the parish church. One day in 1952, a visitor calling to the presbytery, which was across the road, said to Pauline, who was standing outside her house, "Could you tell me where Father Willie Murphy lives?" The man was none other than the great, Bing Crosby, who happened to be a friend of Father Willie. Pauline offered him her autograph and he said that's why he came to Ireland!

On the Avenue, the next house was Mr. and Mrs. Flanagan and their family, Patsy and Rene. Mr. Flanagan worked as a baker in Blackrock College. Indeed, during the war when it was impossible to buy a white loaf of bread, Mrs. Flanagan often dropped a white loaf into my mother which was much appreciated by all the family.

Next door to the Flanagan's were Mr. and Mrs. Michael Howe. Mrs. Howe was known locally as Granny Howe. She was later joined by her son Michael and his family who came from Listowel, Co. Kerry. Mr. Francis Graham, a dairy farmer, lived in Number 79 which was called Sunnyside at that time. Mr. Graham had his dairy in Blackrock. His niece, Margaret McGahon is now living in the parish, with her husband, Donal at 130 Rock Road; they are both involved in parish activity; Margaret with the social committee and Donal with the communications committee. They have both been very helpful to me with bits of information and photographs for this book and I thank them for that.

Now, let us go into Pembroke Cottages; in No. 1 Mr. and Mrs. Jim and Kitty Healy lived with their family, Richard (Richie) Terry, Rita, Nolleen, Brendan and Jim who was a tram conductor and a great character. He used to say to the ladies boarding the tram: "Did you McClean your teeth this morning, Madam?" He would shout out very loud when the tram stopped at Booterstown (Booterstown Avenue).

One day, when I was about six years old, Richie put me into a pram; he ran down the middle of Booterstown Avenue, jumped onto the side of the pram and we careered down the Avenue, straight across the road at the tram lines and on down the Station Road – I would not like to chance that now; we were going to the dump to pick coke and wood for the fire.

Richie was very like Danny Kaye – did you see him in the film *Hans Christian Anderson?* – fantastic! Well, we used to see Richie in the front room of his house, at the mirror, combing his hair, saying to his little sister, "Who am I like, Nono?" She would reply, "Danny Kaye, Richie."

In house No. 2, Pembroke Cottages lived Mr. and Mrs. Stapleton with their son, Eddie and their daughter, Jenny. Eddie joined the IRA and practised drill and army training in the Dublin Mountains. When it was getting near to Easter 1916, Eddie decided he had had enough of it; he didn't turn up to any more training, so two IRA men came to Eddie's house and gave him twenty four hours to leave the country. The poor, inoffensive man, who wouldn't hurt a fly, had to go to Scotland, where he stayed for five years, before returning. House No. 3 was home for the Dunphy family – Paddy, Gin, Min and Liz – they were very, old-world people. Liz liked to smoke, but her brother Paddy said it was a filthy habit and he wouldn't allow any of his sisters to smoke. So Liz, who spent most of the day at the side door of the house greeting people as they passed by, used to ask them where they were going and what they had in the bags they were carrying. She would smoke a few cigarettes during the day, if she had no cigarettes she would call one of the children, who were playing outside and say to them, "Run quick, fly, gallop, you know what I want, two, put them on the window and ill give you something tomorrow." She wanted two cigarettes, so whichever of us she asked, would go to the shop, with the one penny she gave us to buy two cigarettes and put them on her window. The next day she would give us a sweet.

In house No. 4 lived Mr. and Mrs. Dolan and their family, Benny, Paddy, Philip (Philly) George (Gorgie) and Esther (Hetty). Mr. Dolan worked as a sailor with the Irish Lights; he was away at sea for six weeks at a time. He was a great craftsman and made furniture, brushes and mirrors with silver adornments. He once showed me how to insert minute, sailing, ships into fancy bottles. In house No. 5 lived Mr. and Mrs. Felton and their daughter, Pat who was an accomplished, Irish dancer. Pat fell in love and married Kevin Burns from Rosemount Terrace; Kevin was a steward and collector in our parish church for many years. In house No. 6 lived Mr. and Mrs. Clarke and their family, Noel, Dermot and Imelda. Indeed, Imelda is still living in the parish, on Booterstown Avenue.

My mother told me that she, Paddy Clarke and some friends played football in Pembroke Cottages around the turn of the century in 1902. There's nothing new under the sun; we were doing the same in the 1940s and today the children are doing the same in the 21st century.

In house No. 7 lived Mr. and Mrs. Mann with their family, Lummy, Beller, Johnny and Mary –who were special characters, in the scheme of things in Pembroke Cottages! In house No. 8 Mr. and Mrs. Bolger lived with their daughters, Rose, (Rosie) and Molly. Mr. Bolger was a merchant sea-man; he was away at sea for long periods. Over the years, he developed a north of England accent. Once, on arriving home, he caught Rosie smoking and said, "Rosie, I caught you smoking, don't tell your dad lies!" I remember one winter's day, we were all sitting around the fire and there was a knock at the door, in walked the Skipper Bolger, as he was known, "Hello Nanny, I just brought you a small gift," he said and opened a case and proceeded to throw small black rocks onto the fire. I thought he was gone mad, as I had never seen coal, but soon the coal blazed up and we had the best fire I had ever seen. In house No. 9 lived Mr. and Mrs. Murphy and their family, Andrew (Andy), Ann and Grandfather Murphy. I often saw Grandfather Murphy walking very slowly to the corner of Pembroke Cottages. He would stand there for about an hour and then slowly make his way back to the house; I often wondered what his thoughts were. A couple of years went by and then he died; apparently, his legs were tucked in, rigor mortis had set in, so the undertaker had to break his legs to get him into the coffin. Andy told me the gory details which we both marvelled at. In house No. 10 lived Mr. and Mrs. Colgan and their daughter, Imelda. Mr. Colgan (Bill) worked in Power's Distillery, along with Paddy Clarke from No. 6. Bill, his wife, Molly and Imelda went for a long walk every Sunday, sometimes to Goatstown and other times to Nutley Lane, as we all did in those days, of no television or radio. In house No. 11 lived Mr. and Mrs. Redmond and their family, Seamus, Monica,

(Mona) Maureen, Eithne, Kathleen, Sean and Sheila. It was a very sociable house to visit; people gathered there to play cards – twenty-fives – at least once a week.

Sean was a special character, as we grew up; even though he was older than us, he played with us and kept a watchful eye on us all, as we played Cowboys and Indians. He was always the sheriff; later on he pumped the organ in the parish church. In house No. 12 lived Miss Hunt; she looked like a character straight out of the novel *Sense and Sensibility*. She wore the clothes of that era, a long, black, dress with a white, lace, frilly, collar. She had an aristocratic stance and appeared to be looking down her nose at you. "Well, what can I do for you? She would ask when we called at her door. "Our ball went into your garden, Miss Hunt. Could you get it for us?" we would say. Then she would reply, "Wait there," and after a long time the ball would be thrown out to us.

Tom Maguire, Sean Redmond (the Sherriff) and Jimmy Griffin circa 1950, on a day trip to Avoca

In house No. 13 lived Mr. and Mrs. Tom Maguire. Tom was Sacristan of Booterstown parish church from the early 1930s to 1962. His wife, Lizzie was a real character, very witty and great fun to be with. Tom often called on us, that is, my brothers and I, to serve Mass for a visiting priest, who had turned up unexpectedly. Usually he would be an American priest, on his holidays who always gave us 'a little something for our trouble'. Next door to them, at No. 14 lived Mr. and Mrs. Tom Lyng and family, Annie, Veronica, Monica, Tommy, Stan, Dympna, Dorothy and Hilary (who were twins), Paschal and Paul.

In the year 1941 my sister, Annie went to Manchester to join the women's army; she was turned down on medical grounds. They told her to go home and see her doctor; she was so disappointed. She then went to Birmingham and got herself a job in a munitions factory. When she came home for a break, she brought me some lead soldiers, which she had made herself. I was very happy with her gift. While she was at home, Annie brought me into town to have this picture taken in Ross's photographic studio.

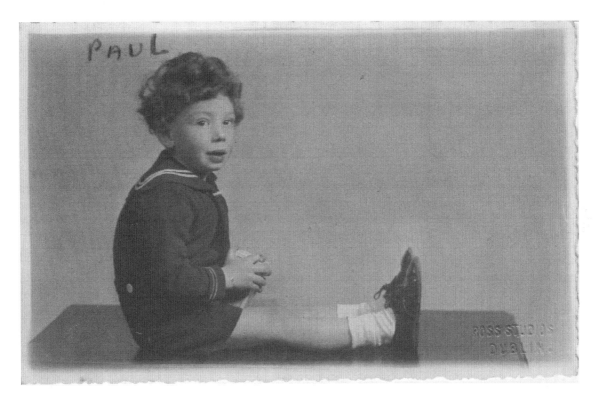

Paul Lyng in 1941

My sister, Veronica went to Belfast to join the Auxiliary Territorial Service (A.T.S.) as many other young ladies did at that time. My sister was accepted and is living in Omagh ever since. Indeed, Veronica has just celebrated her 90th birthday on the 17th of October, 2010 in the Silver Birch Hotel, which was built on the same site as the army camp where Veronica was originally, stationed in Omagh.

My sister, Monica went to work in Bradmola in Blackrock along with many other young ladies at that time. My brother, Tommy went to work with my dad in the pawnbrokers in Amiens Street; incidentally, Tommy wrote a book about pawn-broking, *Bankers to the People*, look out for it; it is a very interesting read. He joined the Local Defence Force (L.D.F.), a popular choice for many young men at the time. My dad was in the Local Services Force (L.S.F) as were many other older men then.

Local Volunteers from the Local Defence Force (LDF)
and the Local Services Force (LSF)

THE ST. JOHN AMBULANCE BRIGADE
IN IRELAND

REVISED SYLLABUS—
A.R.P. COURSE

JANUARY, 1940

Name M.rs A. C. O'Neil.

Address 10, Maretimo Villas,

Blackrock, Co. Dublin.

The St. John Ambulance Brigade in Ireland,
66 Great Strand Street

Syllabus for air raid personnel, January 1940 (front page)

JANUARY, 1940.

Lecture.	Subject.	A.R.P. Handbook.	Section.

1	Introduction.
	Methods of attack from the air and their effects—
	    High Explosive Bombs.
	    Incendiary Bombs.
	    War Gas—
	      (a) Bombs.
	      (b) Spray.
	    Machine Gun Bullets.
	    Panic.
	Danger from bursting Anti-Aircraft Shells.
		9	Introduction

2	Nature and properties of war gases—
	What is meant by Gas ... ...
	Divisions of War Gases into two main groups ...
	    (a) Persistent.
	    (b) Non-persistent.
	Effects of weather ... ...
	Effects produced by Gas on Personnel ... ...
		1
		1
		
		1
		1
			1
			1
			
			2
			3

3	Types of more important Gases ... ...
	    (a) Tear Gases.
	    (b) Nose Gases.
	    (c) Lung Irritant Gases.
	    (d) Blister Gases.
	Characteristics of Blister Gas ... ...
	Detection of Gases (various types) ... ...
	Chemical Indicators ... ...
		2
		1
		
		2
		1
		1
			2
			4
			
			5
			7, 8
			9

4	Protection of the eyes and lungs— Civilian Respirator ... ... Care of the Civilian Respirator ... ... Inspection of the Civilian Respirator ... ... Civilian Duty Respirator ... ... Service Respirator ... ... Care of the C.D. and Service Respirators ... ... Inspection of the C.D. and Service Respirators ... Disinfection of the Civilian Respirator ... ... Disinfection of the Civilian Duty Respirator ... Disinfection of the Service Respirator	1 1 1 1 1 1 1 1 1 1	13 14 15 16 17 18 19 App. D. App. E. App. F.

5	First Aid and Nursing for non-blister Gases—
	    (a) Tear Gas ... ...
	    (b) Nose Irritant Gas ... ...
	    (c) Lung Irritant Gas ... ...
	Injuries produced by Blister Gas ... ...
	First Aid for Blister Gas ... ...
	Anti-Gas Treatment of Persons ... ...
	Nursing of Blister Gas Cases ... ...
	Notes on Mustard Gas and Lewisite ... ...
		2
		2
		2
		2
		2
		1
		2
		2
			2, 18
			3, 19
			4, 20
			6
			7
			25
			21
			8

LECTURE.	SUBJECT.	A.R.P. HANDBOOK.	SECTION.
6	Fitting of Civilian Respirator	1	App. A.
	Fitting of Civilian Duty Respirator	1	App. B.
	Fitting of Service Respirator	1	App. C.
	Poisonous substances not likely to be used as offensive agents—		
	(a) Carbon Monoxide	2	10
	(b) Nitrous Fumes	2	11
	(c) "Paralysing" Gases	2	12
	(d) Phosphorous Burns	2	13
7	Drill—Service Respirator		
8	Protection of the body—		
	(a) Need for protection of the skin against Blister Gas	1	20
	(b) Anti-Gas Clothing	1	21
	(c) Patterns of Anti-Gas Garments	1	22
	(d) Use of Anti-Gas Garments	1	23
	(e) Order of dressing and undressing	1	24
	Preventive cleansing for members of A.R.P. Services	1	26
	Cleansing Depot for A.R.P. Services	1	App. H.
9	Incendiary Bombs	9	Chps. 1, 2, 4
	Decontamination of Materials, General Principles only—		
	What decontamination involves	4	4
	How to deal with non-persistent gases	4	5
	Methods of decontamination for persistent tear gases	4	6
	Contamination by Blister Gases	4	7
	Principles of decontamination for Blister Gases ...	4	8
	Methods and materials used in decontamination for Blister Gases	4	9
	Decontamination of clothing	1	27
	Decontamination of respirators	1	28
	Decontamination of stretchers	1	29
10	General anti-gas precautions and protection of buildings against Gas—		
	(a) How to avoid becoming a casualty ...	1	10
	(b) Precautions for those out of doors in a gas-contaminated area	1	11
	Collective protection in buildings—		
	(a) How to choose a refuge room	Handbook on the Protection of the Home.	
	(b) How to prepare a refuge room against the entry of Gas		
	(c) How to prepare a refuge room against the effect of explosive bombs		
	(d) Things to have in the refuge room ...		
	A.R.P. Casualties Organisation, general scope—	2	15
	Combined wound and gas casualties	2	16
	Organisation of a First Aid Post		
	Sections for dealing with contaminated cases ...		
	Sections for dealing with un-contaminated cases ...		

Syllabus for air raid personnel, January 1940 continued

Now, my brother, Stan was too young to join any of these groups; he was just 14 years of age, so he got his brother, Tommy's, birth-certificate – as Tommy was two years older than he – and went to join the Irish Army. He was accepted and came home in his new uniform; all hell broke loose. My mother was having none of it! But, my dad intervened, saying, "If he's not able for the army they'll find out soon enough and send him home, if not it'll make a man of him." So my mother relented and let him go.

I was fast asleep in my bed on 31st May, 1941. I woke suddenly and wasn't sure why I had woken up. Then the air-raid siren came on in Blackrock College and pandemonium broke loose in our house. My brother, Tommy jumped out of bed and got dressed in his uniform. All the family got up. My dad was in his uniform, Tommy got his gun out from behind the window shutter, where he thought he had it hidden but we all knew it was there. My dad and Tommy went out into the night; both our clocks had stopped at 1.45 a.m. The air-raid siren was still sounding off, we could hear a plane circling around overhead, my mother said, "All back to bed and go asleep." I thought to myself, you must be joking, after excitement like that, I might never sleep again! I did sleep though. The next day, we got the news that the Germans had bombed Dublin and there was nothing left. My mother always said, "I told you a trillion times not to be exaggerating."

In the year 1944, I was standing outside my house, wondering what I would do when five men, brandishing sticks came running towards me. They shouted to me to run; one of the men caught me by the hand and I ran with him onto the Avenue as far as Murphy's pub, we turned around and looked back, a big and very, cross, bull came out onto the Avenue. He stopped and looked around snorting and puffing, the men ran at the bull and he ran back up Pembroke Cottages. I ran with them and as I reached my house, my mother caught me – excitement over!

At this time, World War 11 was at its height. (I have recently been watching a programme on television called *Spirit level* presented by Joe Duffy. Joe was interviewing a man called Tomi, who was a survivor of the holocaust in Belsen Concentration Camp. He described the horrible experience he had, as a nine year old boy. I'm just contrasting my own experiences as a young boy and thinking, how blessed we all were here at that time. My heart goes out to Tomi, his family and all the people who suffered at that time).

My sister, Veronica got married to an army man, Paddy Muldoon. She was engaged to Paddy in 1942 and he was shipped off to the war-zone in Burma. He was involved in jungle-warfare there, for almost two years. My sister and Paddy got married in the Sacred Heart Church in Omagh in the year 1944; none of the family could attend the wedding, because of the very, high security at the border, so my sister and her new husband came to Dublin immediately, after the wedding.

Paddy Muldoon and his wife, Veronica (Lyng)
on their wedding day in 1944

It was great excitement for all of us. My brother Paschal and I went to meet them off the tram at Booterstown; we thought they'd never arrive; we counted seven trams and at last they arrived. We were very happy to see our sister and Paddy, who fitted into our family, very well and was great fun to be with. They now have three children, Bernadette, Tommy and Isabelle.

This time, during the war years was called the Emergency, because everything was in very, short, supply. Each member of the family had a ration book of coupons, which allowed them a certain supply of essential goods. My mother took charge of all the ration books and used them for the shopping each week. The gas company cut down the gas supply after breakfast dinner and tea each day. They could not switch it off completely, because it was considered dangerous, to do so. It was left on a glimmer but it was forbidden to use the glimmer. There were inspectors who did spot checks, they were known as the glimmer-men. One day in 1944, the glimmer-man called to our house – my mother knew him – he was Mr. Dunne from St. Helen's Road; the kettle was just boiling on the glimmer, so my mother kept the glimmer-man talking at the door while my sister made plenty of noise with the sweeping brush out in the kitchen, to distract him. After what seemed an eternity, to my mother, Mr. Dunne said he had to go. As he was leaving, he said to my mother, "I hope you enjoy your cup of tea, Annie."

My sister, Annie had come home from England at this time, as she wasn't feeling very well. She said that she was just a bit tired and she would take a rest for a while before going back to work. Annie was an accomplished pianist, she could teach music and piano technique. Every day she played for us and we enjoyed listening.

Mr. and Mrs. Tom Lyng on their wedding day,
31st October, 1917

My parents were married on 31st October 1917. Every year they had a party on their anniversary. In 1944 they had their usual party and Annie played the piano all evening. Some neighbours were in; glasses of wine were consumed and half-sets were danced. Tom

Maguire and his wife, Lizzie danced a half-set with my mother and Christie Mann. My dad was quite contented to watch, along with the rest of us – a great evening was had by all!

Sadly, it was the last time that Annie played the piano; she became very ill after that. Up until then, she had never told my mum and dad exactly, why she had been turned down for the army. They had discovered she had a congenital heart defect and there was nothing they could do to cure it. Annie wanted to live as normal a life as possible, for the time she had left, and so she didn't say anything about her illness.

Annie Lyng and friend, Mr. Christy Mann

After the party, she went into St. Michael's hospital in Dun Laoghaire, the heart specialist told her everything she wanted to know – and she wanted to know everything – he told her the valves in her heart were defective and that she didn't have very long to live. She took this news very, calmly; she was quite resigned to die.

I was in the garden playing on 26th January, 1945, a sudden fear came over me and I ran in to my mother. She was reassuring me, when there was a knock on the door. Sergeant Kelly, who lived with his wife, in the lane beside Fitzell's shop had called to say that Annie had passed away. My mother couldn't take it in. She said, "It's only an hour since I was with her and she seemed all right then." But it was true, Annie had passed away. This was a sad time for all the family. Now, of course, there is a relatively simple operation to repair or replace the valves in the heart, but not then. Annie was only twenty seven years of age when she died.

My sister, Monica got married in June, 1944 to Paddy Gilligan, from Ballycumber in Offaly; it was a great occasion. They got married early in the morning in our parish church and the wedding breakfast took place at home. We had a great time with lots of music and dancing. They now have four children Sean, Brian, Marian and Padraig.

The happy couple, Paddy Gilligan and his wife, Monica (Lyng) at their wedding breakfast held in the rear of No. 14 Pembroke Cottages, June, 1944

The weddings of my two sisters, Veronica and Monica and the end of the war, in June, 1945 helped to ease the pain of my sister, Annie's death. There was great joy everywhere but the hardships remained and it was a very slow process, getting back to normal.

My brother, Stan was demobbed out of the Army. He got a sum of money, called a gratuity, from the Army, so he bought a Ford V8 truck, which needed some repairs. As he had graduated from the Army Motor Squadron as a motor mechanic he carried out the repairs himself and then started selling turf in the neighbourhood from the back of the truck. The market was good so he continued and my brothers, Hilary and Paschal and I, helped him out. We used to get up out of bed, each morning at 5.30 a.m. and load empty and sometimes, very wet, sacks onto the truck. Stan drove us to the Phoenix Park and at the Park Gate entrance he drove onto a weigh-bridge. There was a small hut beside the weigh-bridge; the man inside the hut took the weight of the truck, then we proceeded onto the turf banks. These banks stretched on, as far as the eye could see.

Stan and Hilary climbed up the rick of turf, Paschal and I stayed at the bottom with both our arms inside the neck of the sack, holding it open with our heads back, as the two boys threw sods of turf, sometimes frozen very hard, into the open sacks. Roughly sixty sacks would be filled in about two hours; it was hard work for grown men – very hard work for young boys.

When the truck was loaded, we drove back to the weigh-bridge. Before reaching the weigh-bridge, Stan would tell us to get out of the truck and go to the other side of the weigh-bridge and wait for him. Thus, when the truck was weighed again, our combined weight was missing from the original weight, which meant Stan had just a little less to pay on his way out and at that time, every penny was precious!

This way of life continued through the very, wet, summer of 1946 until the end of August; the farmers were in danger of losing the harvest so there was a call for volunteers to try to save the harvest. Army trucks arrived in our parish to collect volunteers of fourteen years and upwards. Paschal and I were out of luck; we were too young, much to our annoyance. With the help of the volunteers, the harvest was saved. Then a very harsh winter set in, at the end of the year; it was snowing on the first Sunday in Advent, 1946 just like in 2010. The snow stayed on the ground until April 1947. Then we were back to bringing out the sacks in the early morning. Our routine was to go up to the Phoenix Park and fill the sacks for deliveries around the parish and further afield before bringing in the sacks, doing some school work and going to bed. 'Good night' for all.

In the summer of 1947 both of my brothers, Tommy and Stan got married. This created great excitement for the whole family; don't forget there was no television and very little radio so events like this were a big deal. Tommy married Ita Byrne from Dun Laoghaire, sadly, Ita died on 5th May, 2010; her funeral Mass took place on Saturday, 8th May, she will be missed by Tommy and all his family, Vivion, Damien, Jean, Ita and Tommy, and by the rest of us, may she rest in peace.

Group Photograph of Tommy Lyng and his wife, Ita's (Byrne) wedding in 1947

Stan married Mary O'Connor, also from Dun Laoghaire and had three sons, Anthony, Colm and Michael and a daughter Nova; both marriages took place in the parish church there. At this time my sister, Dorothy entered the Mercy Order as a Postulant. She went to their house in Callan, Co. Kilkenny. After spending a year there, she became homesick and returned home. After a while she entered the Order of the Little Sisters of the Poor in Kilmainham; she stayed two years and then left. She then went to work with Miss Forest in Dublin city, making altar cloths and priests vestments. She later married William Stowe and they had five children, Jim, Anne, Francis, Martin and Niamh.

We now move on to Gardener's Row (now called Rosemount Terrace). Here there were two tenement houses; the people who occupied them were Jemmy Cunningham, a World War 11 veteran, who was shell-shocked. He had a very fine pocket watch and sometimes, as a joke, we would ask Jemmy the time. He would take out his watch and show it to us and say, "Now there's the time." He expected us to say the correct time, as it was on the watch. But, if it was two o'clock, we would say, "Oh! Its five o'clock, already," and Jemmy would say, "It's time for me to go in for my tea." It was a very cruel joke to play on the poor man, but we didn't mean to hurt him. He blessed the four corners of his room every night before going to bed; he also had four bolts on his door. One of the other rooms was occupied by Biddy Williams. Biddy was a very, hard-working woman, she worked in both schools, cleaning every day; she scrubbed the wooden floors once a week and scrubbed floors in the parish church for Confirmation once a year; she always looked unwell. Another room was occupied by Mr. and Mrs. Keenahan and their son, Noel and daughter, Ann. Noel was an altar server in our parish church. The next house was occupied by the Lindsey family who lived upstairs. Mr. Lindsey did very fine boot and shoe repairs; he opened a shoe repair shop on George's Avenue in Blackrock, at a later time.

Mr. and Mrs. Danny and Agnes Hogan and their daughter, Mary lived downstairs; Danny was a courier with C.I.E. tours. He had a great rapport with the tourists, was very witty and also very charming, with a great knowledge of his subject. Living in the room opposite Danny was Sis Brine; she wore a veil to hide the many scabs that covered her face. She was almost blind as well. My friends and I, on a winter's evening would sometimes look into her window where the eerie light of the oil lamp would make our hearts race. When she moved towards us we would run away like the wind, scared out of our wits. When I look back on these encounters, I feel very sad; this poor, old, blind, woman must have been terrified by our actions, even though we certainly didn't mean her any harm.

These houses had one water tap and one outside toilet to serve all the tenants: it was worse for the people upstairs, as they had to carry their buckets of water up the stairs.

Now, we go to Rosemount Terrace, where Mr. and Mrs. Alfie Burns and their family, Tommy, Arthur, Alfie, Kevin, Angela and Maeve lived. Alfie Senior was a veteran of the First World War as was my uncle, Martin; these two men were friends. When they were in the middle of a battle-field at Verdun in France they spotted each other, amid the raging battle, ran towards each other and hugged and danced and hugged each other. What's this you ask? – A touch of humanity in the middle of a battlefield – unheard of!

The two men were wounded later on in the war; they were shipped back to a hospital in

Birmingham and that was the war over for them, thank God! Next door, to the Burns, lived Mr. and Mrs. O'Connor and their daughters, Sheila, and Una. Then there were Mr. and Mrs. Martin and their daughter, Letty and son, Jim. During the Emergency, everything was in short supply, including money. One day the insurance man called to the Martins, looking for his weekly subscription. Mrs. Martin sent Jim out to answer the door; Jim did what he was told and said to the insurance man, "Me mammy told me to tell you she's not in." The insurance man looked into the hall and there was Mrs. Martin hiding behind the curtain, in the hall, but her feet were visible. He replied to Jim, "The next time your mother goes out tell her to take her feet with her!"

Mr. Jim Hughes also lived along here; Jim is remembered for his motor bike with its side car. Tragically, Jim was killed in an accident outside Gleeson's pub in the early 1960s. Living with Jim was his nephew, Joe Gallagher, who was well known to all of us, at that time. In house No. 8, Mr. Ben and Mrs. Rose Ryan and their family, Laurence, Kaye, Aiden, Gerry and Dermot (who were twins), Stan, Rosemary and Veronica lived. Gerry has worked in Gleeson's, as a first class bar-man, for a long time. Gerry told me that in the mid 1950s his father sold No. 8 Rosemount Terrace to ESSO Petrol Company for two hundred and nine pounds. Wow! The company was knocking down a house in Sandymount to build a new service station, so they had to buy a house for the occupant, Mr. Jimmy Deeny. That's how Jimmy came to be living at No 8.

Now, let us move on to the Medical Missionaries of Mary, where Michael Byrne was working and living, Michael was the first person in our parish to receive a Benemerenti Award. He also received an award for fifty years working on the land. Michael was a collector and steward in our parish church for more than fifty years; he was also involved with the Legion of Mary with Jimmy Griffin, Joe Dalton, my father, Tom Lyng, Bob Reynolds and many others. The Legion of Mary also started the first parish youth club at Gardener's Row in the unoccupied houses in the year 1948.

The Medical Missionaries of Mary was founded by Mary Martin; they came to Booterstown to Colonel French's house in the year 1937, Mary Martin was known in Booterstown as Mother Mary Martin, M.M.M (Medical Missionaries, of Mary) the three Ms. Mary Martin also had her sister, Ethel living with them in one of their houses. Ethel was a member of the parish altar society in the 1950s and 1960s.

We now move to McCabe Villas where Mr. and Mrs. Laracy lived in No. 1; they were lovely, old-world people, and they gave a donation towards one of the Stations of the Cross in our parish church in the year 1945. Then there was Mr. and Mrs. Sullivan and their family, Eddie (Mocky) and Paddy.

In the early 1970s, I was sent on a course to Motor Distributors on the Naas Road. It was to introduce us to a new vehicle, the D.K.W. N.S.U. from Auto Union, now known as the Audi motor company. There were people from all over Ireland on this course as well as the man who sat next to me, Joe Dowling, who was originally from Kilkenny but then lived in Manila in the Philippines. We all had to introduce ourselves to the class; when I sat down Joe said to me, "Do you know Mocky Sullivan and Billy Guy?" I was almost blown away; the story goes: Joe got a job in the Convent of Mercy, in the year 1947; it was his first trip to Dublin, so Eddie (Mocky) was sent to meet Joe at the tram stop at the end of Booterstown Avenue. That was their first meeting. Joe continued working at the convent until 1949. Then he emigrated to America – New York, to be precise – where he learnt his trade in the motor industry. He then joined the Maryknoll religious order and became a Christian Brother, he was sent to Manila to teach motor engineering in the technical school there. He was home for a break, had heard about the course and was accepted and then sat down beside me!

Joe came out to see us in Booterstown, paid a visit to the convent and went to see Eddie Sullivan and his family and Mrs. Guy and her family; Billy had passed away some years earlier, R.I.P. Both of the Sullivan boys were great workers and good fun to be with.

Mr. and Mrs. Jennings and their family, Sean, Peter, Mary and Betty lived here also, as well as Mr. and Mrs. Clack and their family. Here also, were two 'famous' window cleaners, George and Charlie; they also had a sister, I think her name was Pauline.

McCabe Villas was also home to Mr. and Mrs. Toddy Heffernan and their family, Tommy, Davie and Betty, who were cousins of mine. Mr. and Mrs. O'Neill and their son, Ginger also lived here and Mr. and Mrs. Murphy and their daughter Patty, lived next door to the O'Neills. Mrs. Murphy was a church cleaner, cleaning the church on her own, for many years. Mr. and Mrs. Guy and their family, Michael, Johnny and Chrissie lived in the next house. Their father, Billy was a great character and a hard worker. He worked for the local, dairy-farmer, John Kenny.

Billy Guy, Chummy Perry, Mocky Sullivan and John Kenny were driven to fields in Rathfarnham at 3.30 a.m. by my brother, Stan, with buckets, stools and a large churn, each day, just as daylight was breaking. They went to the fields to milk the cows and came back to Booterstown to cool the fresh, hot, milk and deliver it to the families around Booterstown at 7.00 a.m.

Mr. and Mrs. Flanagan lived here with their daughter Dolores and son Matt, who was a bicycle mechanic; he worked with sleights for many years. Also living here were Mr. and Mrs. Potts and sons, Michael, Willie and John and their sister, Josie. Michael, Willie and John, were prominent members of the Catholic Boy Scouts of Ireland. Mrs. Parsons and her daughter, Amanda also lived here as well as Mr. and Mrs. O'Keefe and their family, Denis, Peter, Margaret, Elizabeth and a son called Champ, who was very, sadly, killed early one morning while he was delivering newspapers on the Stillorgan Road. He was only 10 years old.

Also living in McCabe's Villas was the Cunningham family. Mr. and Mrs. Cunningham had 11 children, John, (Scissors) Brid, Joe, Mary, Pauline, Kevin (Danno) Ellen, Brendan, Billy, Paddy and Kathleen. John was the first 'teddy boy' in Ireland; we were all amazed when we saw him at first; we thought he was gone mad, but the style soon caught on – the Edwardian style: Long velvet coats; drain pipe trousers; side burns; winkle picker shoes and a special hairdo called a DA (Duck's Ass)!

Scissors was a fantastic rock and roll dancer, so he teamed up with a girl called Kay Jenkins from Dun Laoghaire, who was equally as good. They had bookings to appear in the Theatre Royal; for some time they had a regular spot with Jimmy Campbell and the Royal Orchestra and were known as – would you believe it? –'Scissors and Kay'. Danno was a milkman; in those early days, he delivered milk around Booterstown, early in the morning. For the people who were slow to get up, he would shout in the letter box, "Early Riser."

Willie Maycock also lived in McCabe Villas; he was a small, blocky, man and had a very large Triumph motor-bike; we all thought he looked funny on his motor-bike. The Kinch family also lived here with their family, Cathleen, Jim, Mick and Paddy, who was a good boxer. Tom Geoghegon was another special character in the area.

Mr. and Mrs. Bob Reynolds and their family were very prominent people in the locality; Bob had a horse and cart; he raised pigs and did general farm work for the Sisters of Mercy. Bob was a member of the Legion of Mary and a church collector. He also managed St. Bridget's football team. Mr. and Mrs. Daly also lived here with their sons, Raymond and Seamus and their daughter, May. Mrs. Kathleen Daly, Mrs. Peggy Quinn and Mrs. Cantwell attended the 7.30 a.m. Mass each morning. From 1976 until a few years ago, I opened the church at 7.00 a.m. each morning and they were always there, waiting for me to open up; God bless them all. Seamus Daly is still living in McCabe's Villas and is a good friend of ours. Mr. and Mrs. McGuinness and their family also resided here as did Mr. and Mrs. Staunton along with their family, Seamus, Leo, Cathleen, Christie and Eileen. Like my sister, Veronica, Eileen Staunton also joined the A.T.S. and played a part in the Second World War. Sadly, Eileen died at the time of writing this book. Her daughter, Jean still lives here with her husband, David and their family. Mr. and Mrs. Stapleton and their family, Hubert, Angela and Thomas also lived here. Indeed, Hubert and Thomas still live here. Mr. and Mrs. Stapleton and their family – Maura, Phyllis, Johnny, Philip, Joe and Tom – are another family still living here.

Mr. and Mrs. Farrelly and their family, Owen, Paddy, Noel, Larry and Jim were well known to all of us when they lived here during the 1940s. Mr. and Mrs. Brady and their family, Maria, Liam and Jimmy were also well known to us. Jimmy was a member of the 29th Dublin Boy Scout Troupe in Blackrock along with my brothers and me; Jimmy went on to qualify as a motor mechanic. I think he emigrated sometime after that. Living here also at that time, were Mr. and Mrs. Gill and their family. Johnny Gill worked for Dun Laoghaire Corporation; he had a hand-cart with a shovel and brush and he kept the whole of Booterstown spotlessly, clean and free of weeds; I wish he was here now!

There were two McKeever families living here at that time; Imelda, Phyllis and Kevin belonged to one of the families – Phyllis married a neighbour, Michael Shelly. The other

McKeever family had two sons, Eamon and Brian, both of whom were accomplished Irish dancers and musicians. Eamon was excellent at playing the accordion and Brian the fiddle. Mr. and Mrs. Brennan and their family, Jimmy, Nick and Sheila also lived here at the time. There were also two Dunne families, at the time, in McCabe's Villas; one a very large family, the other a smaller family. Mr. and Mrs. Dunne of the larger family worked for Dun Laoghaire Corporation. The family, as I remember, were Tom, who was a great runner in South Co. Dublin, Anne, Betty, Joe, Damien, Maureen, Peggy, Veronica and Michael (Chum), who sadly, died on 31st May 2010, R.I.P. The other Dunne family had Teddy, Eileen, Maisie, Willie and Pat. This Mr. Dunne was a baker in Blackrock College.

Mr. and Mrs. McDonald and their large family also lived here; Maura and Sheila are the only ones of the family that I can remember. Mr. and Mrs. Perry lived here as well with their family, George, Chummy, Mary and Josie. Mr. and Mrs. Mulvany and family also came to live here, having lived at the lodge in Sans-Souci beforehand. When the Christian brothers took over Sans-Souci, Mr. Peter Mulvany became their farm manager.

Mr. and Mrs. Kinsella and their family, Ian, Noel, Dave, Tommy and their sister, Stella also lived in McCabe's Villas. Tommy played for Shamrock Rovers. Mr. and Mrs. Bunty and Hannah Kelly and her family, Jimmy, Maura and Bridget were also here at that time. They were lovely characters and great fun to be with. Mr. and Mrs. Michael Cullen lived here with their family, Jenny, Cora, Michael and Noel.

The Doyle family lived in the lodge at the entrance to Collegne's House; the Collegne's were running a pig farm at that time, later on the Carroll's ran the farm. The Doyle family were well known to us all, especially Tommy who was married to my cousin. The gate and lodge are long gone; they were directly opposite the entrance to McCabe Villas.

Mr. and Mrs. Dalton also lived here with their family, Christie, Joe, Val, Cathleen, Phyllis and May. Christie and Joe were members of the L.D.F. During the war years they both took part in a military tattoo in the R.D.S at Ballsbridge. Joe was a member of the Legion of Mary and a founder member of the first youth club in Booterstown. He was also a steward and a collector in our parish church for at least 55 years. Joe Dalton, Desie Murphy, Kevin Sheldrick and Kitty McHale all received the Benemerenti Award about two years ago.

Mr. and Mrs. Brennan and their family also lived here in the 1940s as did Mr. and Mrs. Hughes with their family, Michael and his sisters. Michael was an altar server and a collector in our parish church; he also joined the L.D.F. and took part in that military tattoo.

We remember Mr. and Mrs. Carr and their family who lived here, Ambrose, Pious, Gerry and especially, their daughter, Kitty who was also a church collector. Also living here at the time were Mr. and Mrs. Pluck with there family Jim, Joe and Rose. Mr. and Mrs. Aylward also had their family living with them here, while in No. 61 was the Daniels family – Mr. Thomas and Mrs. Bridget Daniels and Annette, Benny, Aiden, Kathleen, Paddy, Patricia and Sean Daniels. Mr. Christopher and Mrs. Christina Mann lived in No. 45 with their family, Christie, Barbara (Babs), Benny, Lily, Paddy and Seamus. Mr. and Mrs. Wolfe lived in No. 65 with their son, Gary and daughters, Annie and Maureen – ah, yes! We remember them well! Mr. and Mrs. Leonard lived in No. 63 with their sons, Thomas (Laddy), Jackie, Liam (Guard) and their daughter, Maureen. Mrs. Leonard had great devotion to the Child of Prague (The Little King). She told me that she always kept a shilling underneath The Little King, so she would never be short of money. Jackie was a member of the 41st Dublin Scout Troupe with my brother Stan, who was the bugler there. Liam was like a rubber ball; he could do all sorts of tumbling tricks; he could stand on his hands and run around in that position, until timb's eve. He was a member of the Maria Mater Fife and Drum Band; he played the big bass drum; you couldn't be blamed for thinking the drum was walking around on its own, because Liam was so small you just couldn't see him behind the drum – that's why he was called 'the guard'.

Liam was also a member of Mr. Nolan's suicide squad with Desie Murphy in Blackrock Tech; they used to somersault over the vaulting horse – the horse was too near the wall, so when the lads did their somersault, they often bore through a very large map of the world that was on the wall – some nights the lads were scraped off the map. We used to say to them, "Where were you tonight lads?" They used to answer, "We were all over the world."

Laddy was a great worker; he drove a truck for McHenry, a coal merchant in the city, delivering coal all over Dublin. He later got a job driving an oil-tanker for one of the oil companies. Laddy also received an award for driving for thirty-five years without an accident. He married Kathleen Redmond from Pembroke Cottages; they had two sons,

David and Thomas. Kathleen and Laddy had a very happy life together; sadly, Laddy died some years ago. Kathleen's two sons are married now with children of their own and Kathleen is still living in what was the Leonard family home, with happy memories of Laddy and the 1940s and 1950s.

Mr. and Mrs. Michael Shelly and their family Joe, Bridget, Maura, Mary, Cathleen, Joan, Phyllis and Michael lived next door to the Leonards. I knew Michael very well; he was a very good footballer and played some very lively games of badminton in the station, bicycle-room with Joe Dalton, presided over by the station-master, Sean Deegan.

At this time, Michael and Joe, like many others of us in the area, used to set night lines in the sea. This involved staking a line on the sand, out on the forth bank with about 50 hooks. Bait had to be dug during the day and then it had to be put on the hooks, as the tide was coming in and you had to be there when the tide was going out. One night at 11.30 p.m. when the tide was going out, Sean Deegan went out with Michael and Joe with a carriage lamp, to look for fish on the line. The last train from San Fernando was just coming into the station. What could be more important – a fish supper, with a few chips, or a train needing attention – from the station-master? That train was a terrible inconvenience!

Michael, unfortunately had to have a lung removed, which stopped him from becoming a great footballer; He fell in love with Phyllis McKeever, they married and had one lovely child, Gina, who is still living there with Phyllis.

Mr. and Mrs. Murray and their family, Joe, Francis, Bobby, Teresa, Margaret and Carmel were living next door to the Shelly's. Joe now lives alone, as all the family has passed away. He works for the council and is a very good worker; they are very lucky to have him. Joe looks after himself and is a very, capable man, God bless you, Joe!

Mrs, Daly, a widow, lived next door to the Murray's with her family, Jack, Dennis, May and Peggy. Next were Mr. and Mrs. Hugh Donnelly and their daughter, Bridie. Hugh worked with Dixon and Hempenstall in Blackrock as a bicycle mechanic. Living in No. 70 McCabe's Villas, were Mr. and Mrs. Kelly with their family, Edward (Eddie), Tommy, Austin, Bridie, Brendan and Paddy. Mr. Kelly was a tram inspector; when the trams finished operating, he retired after a very short while. Paddy (The Professor) and I went to school together to the Christian Brothers' school in Dun Laoghaire; we were in the same class. When I would be walking down to school in the mornings, Paddy would run past me in an awful hurry with his hands gripping the straps of his school-bag, running like the wind. Coming home from school, he would jump off the tram at the Punchbowl and run all the way home. We had a story in our English reader called 'The Hungry Runner', so we christened Paddy 'the hungry runner'; he passed away a few years ago, may he rest in peace.

Another man I remember very well is Jack Connell; he used to sing at the evening devotions and the monthly sodality in our parish church. At a later time, Jack moved away from McCabe's Villas and the last I heard was that the poor man was murdered, may he rest in peace.

We now move back to the corner of Willow Place on Booterstown Avenue. Mr. and Mrs. John C. Russell lived here with their son, Jack and their daughter, Jane. Jack has a corner in Gleeson's pub, named after him. Next door, living in No. 48 were Mrs. Bourke and her son, Daniel – who was a bit strange – he met my dad on the Avenue one day and said, "Listen here, bing, sting, lyng, ging, I am going to report you to the Archbishop of Dublin for running a brothel on Dorset Street." My dad couldn't help laughing about it, it was so absurd. Another day, down at the railway station, my dad was waiting for a train; along came Bourke, he had spotted that my dad had a calendar with Blessed Martin de Porres on the cover. He said to him: "Eh, Lyng, is that sugar, Ray Robinson?

One day I was in the sacristy of the church, waiting to serve Mass. Canon Flanagan was vesting; suddenly, the door was flung open, it was Daniel Bourke. He said, "Listen here, Flanagan, you're three minutes late starting Mass, get a move on."

Next door at No. 50 Willow Place lived Mr. and Mrs. Martin Bourke – no relation to Daniel. Martin Bourke was a member of the Police Force; he had a section of bog up on the Feather Bed Mountain; during the summer, he used to cut and dry the turf and in the autumn, he would bring the turf down in a large truck. Then, he would gather the boys and girls in the area, to bring in the turf in wheel barrows, baths and any container we could get our hands on. When all the turf was in, we would get lemonade and a sum of money each.

Next door in No. 52 is the presbytery, where Fr. Daniel Lucey lived. During the bad winters, we, the children of the neighbourhood, used to shovel the snow away from the footpath in front of his house and he would bring us in and give us lemonade and apples: Wow! We were so full of lemonade! No. 54 (St. Mary's) was where Sarah Chandley lived. In the mid-1800s Monsignor Ford and the Reverend John Ennis lived there and in the 1940s, the McDonagh family came to live there, where Marjorie looked after her blind mother and her two brothers – they were both altar servers in the parish church.

Mr. and Mrs. Billy and Kay Costelloe and their family, Jack, Eleanor, Cinnia, Mairead, Michaela, Robert and Paul, had a stable at the rear of the house, with access from Willow Place; they also had a field at what is now Willow Mount where they kept some lovely horses. We often saw them all going down to Merrion Strand to gallop the horses for exercise. Of course, Merrion Strand was no stranger to horse traffic; they used to run races there at one time; I don't know if the Costelloe's took part in these events. When Robert (Robin) was about ten years old, it was discovered that he had a hole in the heart. In the 1950s they were beginning to make a lot of progress with this kind of medicine, so when Robin was about 14 years old, his mom and dad, Billy and Kay, brought him to America to have open heart surgery, to repair the damage. It was one of the first operations of this kind in the world; we were all very glad it was a complete success. Robin went on to become a very successful architect; sadly, when he was at the height of his career, he was killed in a car accident on the Stillorgan Road. It was a big shock for all the family and all the neighbours.

As you all know, his brother Paul Costelloe has gone on to reach the top of his profession in the fashion world and I wish him well. The next house was called Kimberly; it was occupied by Mr. and Mrs. Francis Smith, a lovely, kindly couple. The next house was occupied by Mr. Robert Cole, and in more recent years by Dan and Mags Sheeran; sadly, they were both killed in a plane crash off the coast of Florida. In the next house Mr. and Mrs. Cole and their family happily lived. Next to Cole's house, was Fitzwilliam Lodge, where Mr. and Mrs. Johnston used to live. Then there was St. Brendan's, on the corner of Cross Avenue; this house was occupied by Mr. John Cruise in 1897 and is now occupied by the Holy Rosary Sisters, who are doing marvellous missionary work, throughout the world. Mr. and Mrs. Ryan lived here with their family in the 1940s; their daughter, Anne is now married to

Aiden Maguire and they are still living in the parish, at the top of Booterstown Avenue. Now, going past Cross Avenue, the first house is St Jude's. Living here were Mr. and Mrs. Keating and their family; their son, John and daughter, Jenny who was a reader in our parish church. Living next door at Rosario were Mr. and Mrs. O'Shea and their family, Pamela, Dorothy and Brian. Mr. O'Shea was a Commandant in the Irish Army. Brian set the town on fire, when he became a film star and took part in a film called *Arms of Clay*. Indeed, Pamela and her husband, Hubert Croghan still live at Rosario.

Next came the allotments – parcels of land, which were used to grow vegetables and potatoes during the Emergency – it is now known as Booterstown Park. Next on the Avenue was a lodge, which was in the grounds of Cherbury House. It was occupied for a time by Tommy and Hannah Behan and after them by Jimmy and Bridie Griffin after they were married. Now, the lovely, eighteenth century house where Lieutenant, Colonel and Mrs. Edgeworth ran a market fruit garden during the war years is no longer standing; they were a lovely, old-world couple. When the fruit was ripe and ready for picking, us, punters from the town, were brought in to pick the fruit. Well, talking about an economic downturn – we ate all the profits; when we were finished there was no fruit to sell – a very, large, lead, balloon! Very sorry, Mr. and Mrs. Edgeworth, its not so bad, they really, only operated the garden as a hobby.

The next house on the Avenue was Weston, where Mr. and Mrs. Doyle were living. This brings us to South Hill Avenue. Miss Janey O'Reilly was living at South Hill Cottage and nearby, at Hamilton Lodge, Mr. and Mrs. O'Neill and their family of eight boys and three girls lived; all the boys played rugby. I remember Willie, Joe and David, especially, Willie, who played for Ireland. I know that Joe was on the verge of getting a place on the Irish team too, but sadly, it didn't happen. It is said that the writer Neville Shutte lived on South Hill Avenue for a short time also.

Mr. and Mrs. Sean Collins lived at Inchydoney at the top of Booterstown Avenue; Sean Collins' brother was the famous republican, Michael Collins; Sean was a regular attendee at the 7.30 a.m. Mass in Booterstown church. In the early 1940s, Canon Flanagan asked for donations for a new set of Stations of the Cross for the church, so Sean paid for the twelfth station in remembrance of his brother, Michael; it is of the crucifixion – is there a message there? Beside St. Joseph's altar in our parish church there is a plaque with the names of the donors.

The next house on the Avenue was Pranstown House; there was a lodge in the grounds occupied by Mr. and Mrs. Tighe – a lovely couple, I don't know who occupied the big house. Around the corner in No. 1 Stillorgan Road, which was called, Ashurst were Mr. and Mrs. William Brudenell-Murphy; they had a butler and eight servants: John Doogan (Butler; aged 28), Mary Kelly (aged 21), Mary Broe (aged 20) Margaret Conroy (aged 50), Annie Conroy (aged 15), Kate Keogh (aged 22), Margaret Monahan (aged 33), Bridget Reynolds (aged 55) and Mary Williams (aged 40).

William Brudenell fell down the stairs and tragically, he died. Mrs. Brudenell-Murphy made several bequests to Booterstown church – two beautiful stain glass windows, the Baptism of the Lord and the Assumption of Our Lady, the marble bust of the Sacred Heart, the lovely large Crucifix in the sanctuary, and the High Altar – Wow!

Now it's back down to the corner of Gardener's Row. Muriel Mathews (Mooie) had her little shop here; she sold cakes and sweets, especially Gur cake; this is a very large slab of fruit cake. I used to go into her shop and ask, "A penny's worth of Gur cake, Mrs Mathews?" I didn't dare call her Mooie to her face. You could be eating this Gur cake for hours and wouldn't want to go for a swim after eating it, because you would sink like a stone!

In No. 83 lived Mr. and Mrs. John Kenny and their family, Jim, Simon, John, Joe, Noel and Paudge. John Kenny was a dairy-farmer and delivered fresh milk all around Booterstown from Shamrock Dairy, at 7.00 a.m. each morning. John had fields rented from the Convent of Mercy and he delivered milk to the convent each day and the convent supplied the parish priest, Canon Flanagan with his milk each day – it was a nice little arrangement! There was a falling out between John Kenny and the sisters, so then they decided to get their milk from Mr. Arthur Davis, another dairy farmer in Booterstown, who just happened to be a Protestant. Well, some time after that John Kenny got the flu and Canon Flanagan paid him a visit. On entering John's bedroom, he said, "Well, John, how are you today?" John answered, "I am not feeling very good, Canon, but I see you're looking horrid well on the Protestant milk."

John Kenny had his haggard where Mrs. Helen Brophy built her house and Montessori School. At that time, it was all fields; there was no school or car park; there were no cars – didn't I tell you that I came out of the ark! I remember running barefoot through the fields, in early May – a lovely field of cowslips; the scent of the flowers filled the air... until, I stepped on a cow pat. That brought me back down to earth again – the moment was over!

What's a haggard? What's a cow pat? I hear you ask. Well, ask your mother! A haggard is a place for storing hay, gathered in from various fields around the parish; it was brought in by a hay bogie – with all us lads hanging on to the back of the bogie – and deposited in the haggard.

Hay bogie

Billy Guy used to be on hand to make the base; from there, the hay was built into a very high rick; there was also a grain pit in the haggard. This pit was filled with grains from Guinness's; a big truck would arrive, full of hot grains. The liquid running out of the grains was porter. Some of the lads would hold their mouths under the porter, but it wasn't very nice to taste.

How do I know that? I'm not telling! When the truck tipped the load into the pit, we lads were all on hand, in our bare feet, to jump into the pit and trample the grains flat – we loved doing this.

One evening in July, we, Georgie and Philly Dolan, Tony Lynch, Andy Murphy, Mal Long, my brother, Paschal and I were playing football in Pembroke Cottages, when Constable Denis Geary arrived. Straight away we all ran away; the chase was on; some of the lads ran towards the Villas, I ran into the haggard, then, I became aware that Geary was following me. I ran past the rick of hay, towards the gate, which led into a field – now the church car park – I dived straight over the gate and rolled up onto my feet; I had a quick look and saw Geary jumping straight over the gate. Wow, an Olympic Champion! There were gates at the entrance to what is now the car park; I quickly went through the side gate, closing it after me to slow him up, and ran into the church and hid in the confession box. My heart was pounding, so loud, I was sure he would hear me. He did come into the church, but he didn't look into the confession box – another escape, for the Scarlet Pimpernel, phew!

The next house was No. 85 where Mr. and Mrs. Tarpey and their daughter, Marcella lived. Right next door was Mr. and Mrs. Mickey Fitzell, who ran a very high class grocery store.

PHONE No. 261 BLACKROCK

M. FITZELL
HIGH-CLASS FAMILY GROCER & PROVISION MERCHANT
87 Booterstown Ave., Blackrock, Co. Dublin
THE BEST OF EVERYTHING ONLY STOCKED
Civility, Cleanliness & Prompt Deliveries   PERSONAL ATTENTION TO ALL ORDERS
Please Call in and Leave a Trial Order ::   :: Satisfaction Guaranteed

Their deliveries went to Galloping Green to the south and to Morehampton Road to the west; they also delivered north and east covering a huge area. It was a very, well laid out shop. Behind the counter there were mahogany drawers, all labelled for different produce; rice, sago, tea, sugar, etc. There were biscuit tins in front of the counter with glass lids, so that you could see what you were buying. We used to ask for "A penny's worth of broken biscuits, Mr. Fitzell?" and he would reply, "Here's two, break them yourself." Bernard Reid was working there for years; he lived in No. 6 Booterstown Avenue. There was a garage in the lane, beside the shop, where Mr. Fitzell kept his potatoes and vegetables, and also the returned, lemonade, bottles and jam-jars. When you returned a lemonade bottle or a jam-jar, you would get a penny for each one returned. There was also a weighing scale in the garage and sometimes they would ask their customers to go to the garage, to weigh their own potatoes. Some of the lads would help themselves to a couple of bottles and jars and return them once again, for a new fee.

At the end of the lane lived Mr. James and Mr. Arthur Davis, dairy farmers; they called their place Primrose Dairy. Arthur also delivered milk in Booterstown. On the same lane, Sergeant Kelly and his wife also lived. It was Sergeant Kelly who brought us the sad news of my sister, Annie's death. Indeed, Sergeant Kelly himself, died not too long after that and his widow, later married Barney Cullen; it was a good match. Sadly, they are no longer with us; they were a lovely couple. The next house on the Avenue is Sydney Lodge. Mr Joseph Woodworth was living here in1901. Now living there, is Reggie Lee and his wife Denise; two lovely and well-known parishioners. The next house was Sans Souci (already mentioned), the lovely eighteenth century, three storey house where Mr. and Mrs. Joseph O'Reilly and their daughter, Jane (Janey) lived until 1937, when they sold it to the Christian brothers and moved to South Hill Cottage on South Hill Avenue. Joseph O'Reilly was chairman of various parish committees; his daughter was a founder member of the parish altar society; she drove her donkey and trap to Mass each day. During the war the L.D.F. used Sans Souci as their headquarters. There were no other houses on this side of the Avenue at that time and it was known as Dark Avenue.

We now move on to Cross Avenue. Living here in No. 1 was Mr. Patrick Keating. In No. 3 was Mr. M. Quish, In No. 5 was Mr. F.C. Hayes, in No. 7 was Kindergarten, Sion Hill and in No. 9 was Abbeyville, Sion Hill. Next was Clareville, Blackrock College. Among the priests there at that time were, President: Reverend, M. Kennedy; Dean: Reverend, T. J. Maguire; Reverend W. Finn; Reverend J. Finucane (Bursar) and Reverend Joseph Corless. Also in residence were Dean of Discipline: Reverend A. J. Hampson, Deans of Studies: Reverend, Dr. David Heelam; Reverend M. J. Harkins; Reverend Cornelius Daly; Reverend P. Meagher; Reverend P. J. O'Shea; Reverend Joseph Baldwin; Reverend C. J. Butler; Reverend Charles Meyer; Reverend James Meehan; Dr. Michael O'Carroll; Reverend Robert Stanley (Stano); Reverend C. Meagher; Reverend F. Mills; Reverend J. Ryan and Reverend C. Murphy. Next door to the college was Dunamase, where Kevin O'Higgins, then Vice-President of the Executive Council and Minister of External Affairs, and his family lived in No. 13.

Kevin O'Higgins: assassinated on 10th July, 1927 on the road, outside the entrance to Sans Souci, on his way to 12 o'clock Mass in Booterstown church.

One faithful morning, he went for his usual swim in Blackrock, after that he was on his way to 12 o'clock Mass in the parish church. O'Higgins sent his personal guard to get the morning paper from Francis Timmons' shop at the end of Booterstown Avenue. On that lovely July day, he saw no danger. As he arrived at Booterstown Avenue, two men were approaching and he smelt danger. He ran towards Sans Souci's side gate; he was gunned down before he reached the gate.

A crowd gathered at the scene of Kevin O'Higgins' assassination,
Booterstown, 10th July, 1927

It was later told, by one of the gun-men's relatives, that he loudly forgave them their terrible deeds, as he lay dying on the road. An ambulance arrived from St. Vincent's Hospital in St. Stephen's Green. O'Higgins would not allow them to take him to the hospital – he ordered them to take him home to Dunamase, where a bed was made up for him in the dining room. Rev. Patrick Dunne, a personal friend, arrived from Haddington Road parish and said Mass for him, as he was dying in his house. O'Higgins died at 5 o'clock on that evening, 10th July 1927.

He was survived by his wife and two daughters, Maeve and Una. Maeve entered the Carmelite Monastery; she took the name Sister Kevin O'Higgins; she is still alive today at the Carmelite Monastery in Kilmacud. To forgive your executioners is the ultimate Christian act, so it is not surprising that Una arranged a special Mass of reconciliation for the 60th anniversary of her father's death on 10th July 1987. Some months before the Mass, the assassins – now dead – had been named for the first time. The Mass was said for Tim Coughlan, Archie Doyle, Bill Gannon and Kevin O'Higgins. The principal celebrant was Professor Enda McDonagh of Maynooth.

Kevin O'Higgins lies in state with guard of honour in the pro-Cathedral, Marlborough St. Dublin

At the Mass was Roger Gannon, the son of one of the assassins. Roger Gannon deposited in the National Archives, a record of his father's account of that tragic event and his dying instruction to his son, to contact the O'Higgins family and tell them how Kevin O'Higgins spoke to them and forgave them, while holding his rosary-beads in his hand.

Bill Gannon, who died in the 1960s, always regretted his part in the assassination. To forgive your enemies is considered a great Christian act; to forgive your assassin is definitely the ultimate Christian act.

At the time of writing this book, Una's great, grandson – Kevin's great, great, grandson, was baptised in our parish church on 31st January, 2010; his name is Hugo Glynn; every good wish, Hugo.

Bellevue, No. 15 was vacant at this time. At The Hermitage, No. 17, lived Mr. Thomas Archer; now Mr, Jimmy Sheehan and his wife Rosemary, live there with their family. Jimmy is one of the leading surgeons in Europe for bone-joint-replacements and he designs and manufactures his own joint replacements, as he is also an engineer. At San Antoine, Mr. and Mrs. Daniel Browne and their family, Aidan, Niall, Donal, Richard, Helen and Kevin who was ordained a priest, in the Spiritan Order in Blackrock College lived. Kevin is so well known to all of us, for his good pastoral work around the parish. At Summerville, No. 21 Mr. Oswald Muller Dubrow was the occupant.

On the other side of Cross Avenue, starting with the Church of Saint Philip and St. James, Rev. Ernest Maunsell Bateman was Pastor and Mrs. Clegg was the teacher in the National School.

Mr. P. F. McCarthy lived next door and the next house was home to Mr. H. T. Chapman. Mr. John Manweiler lived in Dunbeg with his wife and family. Mr. E. Kearon and his family lived in Glenvar House. The Larkin family were living at Larkfield. Doris Larkin was a member of the altar society and in the year 1987 she lovingly and expertly restored the sarcophagus – we still use this for the altar of repose at Easter time.

At No. 2 lived Mr. Thomas Monks. Mr. and Mrs. O'Sullivan lived at Springville with their family, Donal and Desmond – both of whom were ordained priests in the Spiritan Order (Holy Ghost) in Blackrock College – and Ivo and Maurice. Ivo is now living in Maretimo, Blackrock. Mr. J. C. Delaney lived at No. 10.

Living in Herberton was Eamon de Valera and his wife, Sinead and their family, Vivion, Mairin, Eamon, Ruairi, Emir, Brian and Terry. Mr. de Valera T.D. was Taoiseach of Ireland and Minister for External Affairs; there was a hut beside the main entrance of his house where the bodyguards were on guard 24 hours a day.

Next door to them, at Chesterfield, lived Rev. Robert Northridge. Sergeant McManus and his wife lived at the lodge in Chesterfield with their six daughters; the sergeant guarded his daughters like a Rottweiler. During these times Chesterfield, Belleview and St. Margaret's ran market gardens to help the people who had no allotments, to buy potatoes and other garden produce, at a reasonable price.

In No. 26 Cross Avenue Mr. S. J. Mitchell lived. No. 28 was home to Mr. and Mrs. Jim

Broderick and their family. In No. 30 was Mr. C. D. Pearson and in No. 32, Mr. and Mrs. O.R. Fenlon and their sons, Dermot and Frank. Dermot was ordained a priest in the Spiritan Order circa 1980. In No. 34 was Mrs. M. Conroy and in No. 36 were Mr. and Mrs. Irwin with their son, Cyril and daughter, Hazel. Cyril is still living there and is not too well at this time, God bless you and every good wish, Cyril; we are all thinking of you in our prayers.

At number 38 there was Mr. Saunders; at No. 40 Mrs. Sé White; at No. 42 Mr. Edward Reynolds and finally, at No. 44 lived Mr. E.W. Johnson.

Moving on to Mount Merrion Avenue there were Mr. and Mrs. Allen and their family – well known to all in the parish. Their daughter was called Anne; their sons were Michael and Brian. Brian was ordained a priest in the Spiritan Order in Blackrock College. Mr. Allen was a very good singer; he always sang with great gusto at the 12 o'clock Mass on Sundays and evening devotions and also at the monthly sodality. Mrs. Allen came to Mass on her bicycle for many years, Micheal was married on one of the Arran islands – Inis Oir – indeed, there was a full-length film of his wedding on RTE television. Micheal played the flute on his way to the church and the people of the island accompanied him, his wife and relations right across the island, dancing and clapping their hands; it was lovely to watch.

Hugh Brady, a well known architect in Dublin met Anne Allen at university. Anne's father said young men shouldn't take out young ladies unaccompanied, until after they were engaged to be married. Hugh took the hint and popped the question, so Hugh and Anne, who is also a qualified architect, got married on 10th February, 1962 and went to live at Bellevue on Cross Avenue, where they raised their family, Sinead, Deirdre, Sorcha and Fergus. Sadly, Hugh died unexpectedly, at the time of writing this book on the feast of the Epiphany, 2009. He will be missed very much by his family and those of us who knew him as a good friend, may he rest in peace.

Next door to the Allen's on Mount Merrion Avenue were Mr. and Mrs. Slowey in Clonfadda House. My brothers, my friends and I used to visit Clonfadda every Halloween; we always got a big welcome and they brought us into the hall, which seemed very big, and asked us to perform for them, so we sang and danced; they were generous with their praise and gave us fruit and sweets; we always enjoyed going there. Mr. Jonathon Goodbody lived at Pembroke House. Lieutenant, Colonel James Egan was also living here at the time.

We now move on to the Rock Road. At the turn of the century there was a row of houses on the grounds of Blackrock College and also two public houses; they were purchased to make more room for the college grounds; the college compensated the occupants by building houses for them on the other side of the Rock Road. At No. 1, Lisaniskea, lived Mr. Pierce Higgins who donated a lovely ciborium to Booterstown parish church, as a memoriam to his wife, who had just died. At No. 7, Phoenix Lodge, lived Miss Buller and at No. 9 John Flynn; at No. 11 J. Kinch; No. 13 Robert Doyle; at No. 15 Mrs. Kelly, No. 17 Albert E. Bayfield; No. 19 J. Fitzgerald; No. 21 Thomas Fogarty; No. 23 James Aspill; No. 25 Mrs. Power; No. 27 Miss Nora Walsh; No. 29 Mrs. Casey and in No. 31 lived J. Leemann, a boot-maker and Thomas Breen, a member of the Austin Stack Céilí Band.

Living on Willow Terrace were Mr. Samuel McKenzie, Miss L. Ellis, Mr. J. Murphy, Miss Florence Bewley and Mr. and Mrs. James Wilmot and their family. Their son, Ronan became a famous actor on stage, films and television, and for a long time he was a reader in our parish church; Ronan was also involved in a committee to start a boys' club, with Desie Murphy, Noel Cullen, Don Kennedy and John Connolly. The O'Neill family also lived on the Rock Road as did the Cahill family; Mr. Philip Corcoran and family; Mr. and Mrs. Billy and Molly Harrison and their family – daughters, Monica, Sarah and Dorothy and sons, Joseph and William (Bill/Billy). Bill's wife died in 2008, R.I.P. Billy was a well-known contractor in the area; sadly, Billy died at the time of writing this book, may he rest in peace. There were also some shops on the Rock Road at this time. Mr. and Mrs. Mullen had a general store; they had a son and daughter Sean and Irene; Mr Mullen was also a member of the Police Force. Mr. and Mrs. Jim O'Connell ran a Post Office and shop on the Rock Road and indeed their son, Jim was ordained a Spiritan Priest and is now in charge of a very large parish in Pakistan.

Mr. and Mrs. Casey also ran a shop on the Rock Road, and indeed, Mr. J. J. O'Neill and Son were carpenters and builders established here. Next to them was Mrs. Kinimont, then came the garage run by Mrs. K. Williams; later it became the Williams and Sterling garage. On the other side of the Rock Road at No. 2 Beninagh was Mr. John Dunne, Solicitor. At No. 4 was

Mrs. Lazenby; at No. 6 Mrs. Sarah Devitt; at No. 8 Somhairle O'Fathaigh; at No.10 Mrs. Tallis; at No. 12 William Mooney; at No. 14 James Wilson and at No. 16 was St. Catherine's High School, Sion Hill.

Miss Frances Hogg also lived on the Rock Road, as did Edmond Kelly and Spencer Kelly, who lived at Rosefield and Mr. Eamon Martin at Sea Fort Lodge.

In the middle of the shops is Emmet Square; my uncle, Thomas Heffernan and his wife, Mary lived here with their son, Jack. Sometime later, Jack married Julia; they had two sons, Tommy and Danny and two daughters, Kathleen and Betty. Jack was a founder-member of a wrestling club which was based in the Martello Tower in Williamstown; they were living at No. 14 and I thank my cousin Cathleen for helping me with most of the names mentioned here, from Williamstown. Living at No. 1 was Ellen O'Neill – nicknamed, 'the warrior' because she was a bit eccentric, very republican, she would shout very, aggressively, "Up the rebels!" and sometimes raise her hand, in salute saying, "Up the red hand of Ulster!" just to annoy everybody. Her brother Joe was also known as 'the warrior'; there was one other member of the family, Barney. In No. 2 were Mr. and Mrs. John Beggs and their son, Tom, who worked in Sion Hill and his brother, Tweedy. In No. 3 lived Mr. and Mrs. Bride Boyd. No. 4 was home to Mr. and Mrs. Murphy; No. 5 Mr. and Mrs. Fitzgerald. Mr. Fitzgerald was the keeper in Blackrock Park; his wife was a cleaner in the local schools. In No. 6 Mr. and Mrs. Mooney lived with their family. Living in No. 7 were Mr. and Mrs. Watts and their family, Chrissie, Mary, Josie and Charlie. In No. 8 were Mr. and Mrs. Hussy; in No. 9, Mr. and Mrs. Doran and their family; in No. 10, Mr. and Mrs. Jim Bagnal. Living at No. 11 was Mr. and Mrs. Hodgens and their family Lizzie, Ann, Pat and Christopher. Living in No. 12 Mrs. Nolan; No. 13 the Masterson family; in No. 14 (already mentioned) the Heffernan family; No. 15, Nelly Donley and Miss McFarnell; No.16 Mr. and Mrs. Slevin and their family, Sean, Liam and Marie; No. 17 the Timmons family; No. 18 Mr. and Mrs. Jim and Delia Murphy; No. 19, the Cunningham family; No. 20, the Donley family; No. 21 the Butler family; No. 22 the Shelly family; No. 23 the Byrne family; No. 24 Mr. Bob Hatton; No. 25 Miss Armstrong; No. 26 Miss Hodgens; No. 28 the Byrne family; No. 29 Miss Hunter; No 30 the Flynn family; No. 31 the Watson family; No. 32 Mr. and Mrs. Gifney and their daughter, Kathleen; No. 33 the Daly family, No. 34 Mr. and Mrs. Hodgens and their family, Pat and Sheila; No. 35 the Corcoran family; No. 36 Mr. and Mrs. Larry Moran and their family; No. 37 Mr. and Mrs. Tonsi Nolan and their family; No. 38 Mr. and Mrs. Tommy McGahan; No. 39 Mr. and Mrs. Kennedy and their family, Don, Jim, Liam and May. Indeed, Don fell in love with my cousin, Kathleen Heffernan from No. 14 – they got married and raised a family of their own, Carmel, John, Denise and Anthony. In No. 40 lived Mr. and Mrs. Hayes and their family; No. 41 was home to Mr. and Mrs. Aspel. Mr. Aspel worked as a tailor in Blackrock College. Next, in No. 42 lived Mr. and Mrs. McFarnan and their family.

Now we move on to Seaford Parade where Mr. and Mrs. Fox were living; Mr. Fox was a well-known insurance agent in the area. Mr. Tom O'Connor also lived here and Mr. Buddy O'Hanlon; Mr. and Mrs. Wilson; Mr. and Mrs. Hickey and their family; Mr. and Mrs. De-Mangeat; Mr. Tommy Breen, who was a member of the Austin Stack Céilí Band. Mr. Ted Murphy, nicknamed 'the fireman' also lived here. Mr and Mrs McHale and their son Des, who was a very good footballer, were living here at that time.

This is a snapshot of the parish of Booterstown in the 1940s.

I met my wife Maureen on 5th August 1959; it just happened to be her birthday; it was Bank Holiday Monday and we are together ever since. It was the best day of my life and the last 50 years have been the best time of my life; I wouldn't change anything and I want to thank her for always being there for me; all those years making me laugh and filling me full of joy.

I also want to thank my two daughters, Michelle and Martina, my three grand-daughters, Hazel, Ava and Alison and my grandson, Eoin and my sons-in-law, Michael and Justin for all the joy they have brought to Maureen and me – thanks for the memories – I also want to thank all the people of Booterstown for their good wishes, and the people who helped me with information for this book.

Paul Lyng receiving a Benemerenti Papal Award, 2009

On Holy Saturday morning, 11th April, 2009 at approximately, 10.30 a.m. the parish priest, Monsignor Seamus Conway advised me I was to receive a Papal Award. I was in shock for the rest of that week; it took me some time to come to terms with the idea of me receiving an award.

I want to thank Monsignor Seamus for thinking of me in this way and for all the hard work he put into getting this award for me, he is really one of the best shepherds this parish has ever had.

I really don't approve of awards, especially for me, so, I would like to dedicate this award to all the people I have mentioned here, who kept the faith alive in this parish, down through the years, especially, my parents, Thomas and Anne Lyng and all my brothers and sisters, and all my relatives; God bless them all.

'Signing of the register'
Paul & Maureen's Wedding, 15ᵗʰ April 1963

Women
in Transition

The MONEE Project
CEE/CIS/Baltics

REGIONAL MONITORING REPORT – No. 6 – 1999

United Nations Children's Fund
International Child Development Centre
Florence - Italy

The UNICEF International Child Development Centre (ICDC), often referred to as the *Innocenti Centre*, was established in 1988 with core funding from the Italian government to serve as a specialized research and training facility. The Centre undertakes and promotes policy analysis and applied research relating to the rights and welfare of children. It also provides training and capacity-building opportunities for UNICEF staff and for professionals in other institutions with which UNICEF cooperates. The Centre is housed within the *Spedale degli Innocenti*, a foundling hospital designed by Filippo Brunelleschi that has been serving abandoned and needy children since 1445.

This Regional Monitoring Report is the sixth in a series produced by the MONEE project, which has formed part of the activities of UNICEF ICDC since 1992. The project analyses social conditions and public policy affecting children and their families in Central and Eastern Europe, the Commonwealth of Independent States, and the Baltic republics.

Earlier Regional Monitoring Reports are as follows:

1. *Public Policy and Social Conditions*, 1993.
2. *Crisis in Mortality, Health and Nutrition*, 1994.
3. *Poverty, Children and Policy: Responses for a Brighter Future*, 1995.
4. *Children at Risk in Central and Eastern Europe: Perils and Promises*, 1997.
5. *Education for All?*, 1998.

Russian as well as English versions of the Reports are available.

Besides benefiting from the core funding to UNICEF ICDC from the Italian government, the MONEE project receives financial contributions from the UNICEF Regional Office for CEE/CIS/Baltics and from the World Bank.

Readers wishing to cite this Report are asked to use the following reference:
UNICEF (1999), "Women in Transition". *Regional Monitoring Reports*, No. 6. Florence: UNICEF International Child Development Centre.

Design
Bernard Chazine
Printed by
Arti Grafiche Ticci - Siena, Italy
© UNICEF 1999
ISBN: 88-85401-43-0
ISSN: 1020-6728

All correspondence should be addressed to:
UNICEF International Child Development Centre
Economic and Social Policy Research Programme
Piazza Santissima Annunziata 12
50122 Firenze, Italy
Tel. (+39) 055.20.330
Fax (+39) 055.244.817
E-mail: (for information)   ciusco@unicef-icdc.it
           (orders)   orders@unicef-icdc.it

www.unicef-icdc.org

Foreword

The countries of Central and Eastern Europe and the former Soviet Union are going through immense changes, some positive, and some painful. The people who are most affected by these changes are the women and children of the region.

This Report from the UNICEF International Child Development Centre, issued in 1999 to mark the 20th anniversary of the Convention on the Elimination of All Forms of Discrimination against Women, focuses on the situation of women since the fall of communism. It finds that many are missing out on the new opportunities created by transition, and many are feeling the adverse effects. However, the Report also finds that women have often responded to challenges with resilience and resourcefulness.

UNICEF is concerned at the early impact of gender discrimination, which prevents girls from fulfilling their potential in school, in the community and, later on, in the workplace. We are concerned about the continuing discrimination against women that excludes them from full participation in society. We see that around the world when women suffer children suffer, too, and when women's rights are respected children have a better life.

The conclusion of the Report is clear. The countries of the region have an unprecedented chance to build gender equality into their new societies and lead the way into the new millennium. Measures to tackle gender discrimination must include the full implementation of the Convention on the Rights of the Child and the Convention on the Elimination of All Forms of Discrimination against Women.

Such measures are essential, for the underlying aims of transition – more humane societies, higher living standards, greater economic freedom, and true democracy – can only be realized through the full participation of women in the process.

Carol Bellamy
Executive Director, UNICEF

Acknowledgements

This Report has been prepared by a core MONEE project team at UNICEF ICDC with contributions and assistance from a large number of other persons. The core team has been composed of Aline Coudouel, Alessandra Cusan, Gáspár Fajth, Roumiana Gantcheva, John Micklewright, and Albert Motivans. Gáspár Fajth is the volume editor of the Report; responsibility for the views expressed herein rests with him.

Nick Manning and Gillian Pascall have provided a concept paper on women-friendly family policies that has been used in various parts of the text. Andrew Newell and Barry Reilly carried out much of the analysis in Chapter 2 and also wrote Box 1.3. The other chapters were originally drafted by Gáspár Fajth and Roumiana Gantcheva (Chapter 1), Albert Motivans (Chapter 3), Aline Coudouel (Chapter 4), Aline Coudouel and Roumiana Gantcheva (Chapter 5), and Alessandra Cusan (Chapter 6). Further important contributions have been made by Martin Raiser and Peter Sanfey (Box 1.3), MaryAnne Burke (Section 1.4), Dominic Harrison (Box 1.7), Gyula Nagy (Box 2.6), Bruce Bradbury (Box 2.1, parts of Section 2.3 and Box 3.2), Ilona Koupilová (parts of Sections 1.3 and 4.2), and Nick Manning (parts of Section 6.2 and Box 6.5).

Jane E. Foy has acted as consulting editor, improving the text greatly and adding many insights. Robert Zimmermann has copyedited the text. Aline Coudouel should also be recognized here, for she has not ducked the bearing of any burdens. Bernard Chazine and his staff are thanked for their work on the design and layout of the Report.

Papers summarizing particular aspects of the situation of women in individual countries have been written (sometimes in conjunction with other individuals) by Jana Hendrichova and Vera Kucharova, Elena and Catalin Zamfir, Vladimer Papava and Elena Chikovani, Theodora Ivanova Noncheva, Ella Libanova, Ülle-Marike Papp, Aleksandra Posarac, Elena Ivanovna Kupriyanova, Sanavbar Sharipova, and Sheila Marnie.

John Donohue, director of the UNICEF Regional Office for CEE/CIS and the Baltics, in Geneva, and Mehr Khan, director of UNICEF ICDC, have provided encouragement and unfailing support. John Micklewright, head of research at ICDC, and Gáspár Fajth, MONEE project officer, have organized the work, with assistance from Cinzia Iusco-Bruschi and Olga Remenets.

The Report has benefited from the help and comments of many UNICEF colleagues, including Mikayel Alexanyan, Steven Allen, Ekrem Birerdinc, Elena Bogdanska, Stanislaw Czaplicki, Ute Deseniss-Gros, Bertrand Desmoulins, Robert Fuderich, Hanno Gaertner, Nora Godwin, Rudolf Hoffmann, Sona Karapetyan, Latif Kengerlinsky, Roberto Laurenti, Serap Maktav, Alexandre Malyavin, Nada Marasovic, Ken Maskall, Eddie McLoughney, Gianni Murzi, Yuri Oksamitniy, Rudy Rodrigues, Elena Selchonok, Alla Solovyova, Simon Strachan, Abdelmajid Tibouti, Boris Tolstopiatov, Stefan Toma, and JoAnna van Gerpen. We remember our colleague, Yves de Roussan, who died tragically while working on issues related to the Report.

Particular thanks go to Sreelakshmi Gururaja and Joan French, Gender and Development Unit, UNICEF-New York, as well as to Rema Venu and Paula Donovan for their help and their comments.

Individuals in other institutions must also be thanked for their assistance, including Ana Maria Brasileiro and Zina Mounla of UNIFEM; Yuri Misnikov and Sharhbanou Tadjbakhsh of UNDP; Chris Jones, Tim Heleniak, Dorota Holzer-Zelazewska, Jeni Klugman, Maureen Lewis, Helen Shahariari, and Dena Ringold of the World Bank; Martin Bobák, Department of Epidemiology and Public Health, Medical School, University College London; France Donnay, UNFPA; Lev Khodakevich, Bernard Schwartlander and Anita Alban, UNAIDS; Martin Raiser and Peter Sanfey of EBRD; Anikó Soltész, SEED (Hungary); Péter Józan and Erzsébet Eperjesi of the Hungarian Central Statistical Office; Mária Neményi of the Hungarian Academy of Sciences, and Mária Herczog, National Institute on Family and Children, Budapest.

Finally, thanks go to Nigel Cantwell, Patrizia Faustini, Patricia Light, Angela Hawke, Andrea Khan, Eve Leckey, Bernadette Abegglen-Verazzi, Anna Wright, and other colleagues at ICDC, many of whom provided enthusiastic help in the preparation and promotion of the Report.

The Report could not have been produced without the participation of the central statistical offices in the countries of the region. (They bear no responsibility for the way data are used or presented in the Report.) Thanks are due for their many contributions (including written papers) to the following persons and to others working with them.

Albania	Milva Ekonomi
Armenia	Juliette Magloutchiants
Azerbaijan	Meri Gardashkhanova, Arif Veliyev
Belarus	Galina Gasyuk
Bosnia-Herzegovina	Hasan Zolic
Bulgaria	Jaklina Tzvetkova-Anguelova
Croatia	Senka Bosner, Ruzica Adamovic, Robert Jurak
Czech Republic	Jaroslav Novák
Estonia	Urve Kask
Georgia	Teimuraz Gogishvili
Hungary	Judit Lakatos
Kazakhstan	Erbolat Musabekov
Kyrgyzstan	Zarylbek Kadabaev, Kuliypa Koichumanova, Elena Loginova, Kalina Risalieva
Latvia	Edmunds Vaskis, Maranda Behmane
Lithuania	Virginija Eidukiene
FYR Macedonia	Marina Mijovska
Moldova	Jana Tafi
Poland	Alina Baran, Maria Daszynska, Zofia Galazka
Romania	Clementina Ivan-Ungureanu
Russia	Vladimir Sokolin, Irina Zbarskaya
Slovakia	Eugen Placintar, Milan Olexa, Aleksandra Petrasova
Slovenia	Tomaz Banovec, Milivoja Sircelj, Joza Klep
Turkmenistan	Juma Durdy Bairamov, Liudmila Ammaniyazova
Ukraine	Viktor Golovko, Helen Paliy
FR Yugoslavia	Dragisa Bjeloglav, Dragana Filippi

Contents